GW00497644

Relational Interventions

Treating Borderline, Bipolar, Schizophrenic, Psychotic, and Characterological Personality Organization

Lawrence E. Hedges, PhD, PsyD, ABPP

Copyright © 2013 Lawrence E. Hedges

Cover design by Afton Palmer

All Rights Reserved

This book contains material protected under International and Federal Copyright Laws and Treaties. This book is intended for personal use only. Any unauthorized reprint or use of this material is prohibited. No part of this book may be used in any commercial manner without express permission of the author. Scholarly use of quotations must have proper attribution to the published work. This work may not be deconstructed, reverse engineered or reproduced in any other format. The entire book in its original form may be shared with other users.

Created in the United States of America

For Daniel Alexander Uribe

Table of Contents

Part I

Introduction: Relational Listening

Opening Challenge

As psychotherapists we strive to be useful to people struggling with life's many problems. But how exactly do we *do* this? We begin by studying the many competing theories of the mind and theories of therapy now available to us and we choose the ones that make the most sense to us. Only much later are we able to realize that our choice of theories actually *expresses what we intend to do in therapy*—that is, how we believe we can best make ourselves useful to our clients.

Further complicating things, we are today beset with a vast array of medicalized descriptions of people—diagnostic categories devised by psychiatrists to justify to the public and to courts of law their choices of medications and other somatic therapies. To the extent that as psychotherapists we get snagged into medical diagnostic thinking, we have also to contend with the diagnostic system's assumptions and biases—thus adding further complexities to our work.

These many theoretical, technical, and diagnostic complications can easily cause us to loose sight of what is truly important in our work—finding ways to make ourselves useful to people. This book deals with *what we can actually do* in psychotherapy to best position ourselves to intervene in people's lives in ways that will be truly helpful to them.

The central tool of all psychotherapies is the transference—by whatever name it may be called. Transference is simply a description of the ways we bring habits of perception and interaction learned in past relationships to bear on present relationships. Psychotherapists, regardless of theoretical or technical persuasion, are always paying close attention to transference though they may conceptualize and work with it very differently.

The moment we understand the centrality of transference in psychotherapy we can also realize that psychotherapy is essentially relational. *That the help we have to offer to our clients is help with relationships.* This insight helps us narrow our focus considerably from a wide range of competing possibilities.

But how do we help with relationships when what the person brings to us is a list of complaints and troubling symptoms? What kinds of interventions can we devise to help with the essential problems that are coming up in their relationships while at the same time empathizing with life's many pressing difficulties? These questions pose the challenge of this book.

Psychotherapy as Relationship

Neuroscience now teaches that we are first and foremost a relational species. That is, modern technologies now reveal that our entire nervous system—including our brains as well as our endocrine, hormonal, and neurotransmitter systems—*actually organize themselves according to what kinds of relationships are and are not available to us in the earliest months of life.* Furthermore, we now know that our brains and nervous systems continue to generate new

7

neurons and new neurotransmitter pathways throughout our lifespan—depending on what kinds of relational experiences we choose to involve ourselves in. These emerging neuropsychological findings make clear that all emotionally intimate relationships—especially the psychotherapeutic relationship—hold forth the possibility of profound and enduring personality change.

Another line of relational research comes from a task force recently organized by the Psychotherapy Division of the American Psychological Association (Division 29) that reviewed thousands of empirical studies and found that the single most consistently important factor determining the overall outcome of all psychotherapies is *the relationship* between the therapist and the client (Norcross 2002). What clients remember years later is not what their therapists said or did, but the relational moments in which they experienced emotional connection with and emotional recognition from a very real person, their therapist (Stern, 2010).

Thus, good professional work in any clinical setting demands a good working personal relationship—whether the individual practitioner acknowledges the power of the relationship or not. Our professional choices manifest our personal ways of relating—in how we think about and perform our work. Some therapists choose to ignore the relational dimension while other therapists choose to focus heavily on what's going on in the relational exchange. But all highly-skilled, seasoned professionals are acutely aware of what's going on in the relationship at all times and are carefully aiming their work into each relational matrix as it unfolds—no matter from which theory or school of therapy they hail.

I think of family therapist Virginia Satir whom I once watched conducting a family therapy session in front of a large audience spontaneously bursting into tears while directly telling a sullen teenager that her feelings were hurt because he thought she was ganging up against him with his parents when she was working so hard to find a way to let him at last speak what he needed to say to them.

I remember behaviorist Joseph Wolpe telling a group of us about a little girl who had been to numerous therapists for compulsively cutting out paper dolls. After a few attempts to get her attention away from the dolls she was cutting, in exasperation Wolpe stood up towering over her and angrily yells at her at the top of his lungs, "Stop cutting out paper dolls!" And she did.

I once watched Alexander Lowen, father of bioenergetics body psychotherapy aggressively provoke a large burly man who had in fact bare handedly killed several people in the course duty in his law-enforcement career to the point that everyone in the room was terrified Lowen was going to get slugged. Lowen got right in his face and was pounding on his chest until we saw the man crumple on the floor in deep heaving tears and pleas for his father to stop beating him.

Each of these gifted therapists—working in their own way—demonstrates perfect relational empathy under the circumstances. Even one of the founders of Cognitive-Behavioral Therapy Aaron Beck, after reviewing the neuropsychological research on relationships describes the crucial importance of relational context and asserts, "The therapeutic relationship is a key ingredient of all psychotherapies, including cognitive therapy.... Many of the basic interpersonal variables common to other psychotherapy (i.e., warmth, accurate empathy, unconditional positive regard) serve as an important foundation for cognitive and symptomatic change" (Beck and Dozois 2011, p. 401). So since relational variables are an essential and unavoidable part of professional work at all levels it behooves us to fine-tune ourselves to the relational question, "what's going on here anyway."

Considering "Lower Level" or "Difficult to Treat" Clients

Traditional *DSM* diagnoses are well-known to all therapists but the more sophisticated, relationally-oriented diagnostic approach of the *PDM* is less well known. In Appendix B I provide a brief overview of the history of psychodiagnostic thinking in this country, but for our purposes here I wish only to use the overall structure of the *Psychodynamic Diagnostic Manual* (*PDM* 2006) which defines *"borderline-level" relating* as between normal/neurotic and psychotic levels of relating. That is:

Higher = normal/neurotic relational issues
Borderline = character relational issues
Lower = psychotic/bipolar/schizophrenic relational issues

Most clinicians today dread working with individuals who might be seen diagnostically as "borderline, bipolar, schizophrenic, psychotic, or character disordered." Furthermore, it is not uncommon for people seen as normal or neurotic under circumstances of extreme stress or when undergoing therapy to "regress" to experience "difficult to treat pockets" of borderline or even psychotic experience. But there is no need for such dread!

The fact is that the personality features involved in "lower level" or "more primitive" mental states are organized in relatively simple relational modes that eventually yield to effective relational interventions. It remains for the treating therapist to grasp the nature of the personality organization or feature involved in order to go with the flow of the forming relationship and eventually to find ways of being with and enjoying the person who is working what might be called early developmental levels.

The central treatment flaw of most therapeutic approaches is that they are content-oriented rather than relationally process-oriented. Most therapists tend to listen to and then attempt to respond to the subjective narrative or the list of concerns or symptoms provided by the client or by some theory of therapy. But the central issues these clients are struggling with are relational issues that have little or nothing to do with the narrations or lists of concerns they can muster regarding their partners, children, bosses, work colleagues, or their physical, addictive, symptomatic, or sexual issues, or their personal histories.

This book will consider the psychotherapeutic relationship with people and aspects of people that have historically been described by the *DSM* and later by the somewhat more enlightened *PDM* with mid- to lower-level relational capacities. But clearly we have outgrown this history and our profession needs new ways to speak about aspects of ourselves and our clients that have become unnecessarily constricted in the process of growing up, aspects of ourselves that are seeking new "relational freedom" (Stern, in press).

Content vs. Process Treatment Approaches

Content-centered therapeutic approaches to borderline-and psychotic-level personality organizations leave the therapist floundering with cognitive, behavioral, dialectical, or other symptomatic issues, which bypass what the client came to treatment for. Why is a content approach so useless with these populations? Because the issues that are giving them trouble originated in such an early developmental period of their lives that there were and still are no words, pictures, or stories to depict the problems—no recognizable content as it were. While some contents may metaphorically point toward deeper issues, more often than not, the words, pictures, stories, and symptoms actually tend to derail the therapeutic investigation.

The struggles of these individuals are predominately relational and therefore manifest in the ways they relate to us and to the therapeutic setting. That is, very often *people cannot tell us what the trouble is, they can only show us by doing it to us, by engaging us in the fray of their inner lives.*

As a foretaste of where I'm going let me say that the central issues most psychotherapy clients are dealing with today have to do with various forms of engagement and disengagement in actual here-and-now relatedness situations. Knowing that we are looking for individual styles of engagement and disengagement makes it considerably easier for a clinician to focus on what is important and to leave the rest of the content—what I call the "clinical chatter or clamor" to the side. We can't, of course, completely avoid or ignore the content because content is the main thing people know to bring to us. So we have to engage as empathically as possible in the stories, symptoms, and issues brought forward—but such empathic engagement is essentially a trust-building and relational information-gathering technique. We don't have to assume that the stories and symptoms we hear are critical to why they are coming to us. Rather, we need to attend carefully to the ways they approach us and then back away. We need to pay close attention to the kinds of interpersonal engagements they draw us into on a regular basis and the kinds of countertransference responsiveness they evoke in us. I will unpack all of these ideas as we go along, but for now you need to know that what we are looking for in learning to be with and to enjoy these otherwise difficult to be with people or aspects of people is how they engage us and how they disengage us. That in, since borderline and psychotic-level issues are fundamentally relational, all people know to tell us about these basic aspects of personality is what's going wrong in their lives and in their bodies at the time. At the beginning of treatment they have no idea that their modes of engagement and disengagement are what's setting themselves up for mental and physical distress. We might even go so far as to say that effective treatment consists of people coming to *actually experience in the treatment situation itself* just how their personal styles of engagement and disengagement limit and set themselves up for relational problems.

As people come to experience themselves in their habitual relatedness modes in relation to the therapist and then to see for themselves how limiting their modes are, they tend toward developing more flexible and less stressful relatedness modes that serve them better in the world and in their bodies. Donnel Stern from an Interpersonalist/Relationalist perspective speaks of "unformulated experiences"—dissociated in both client and therapist—that become mutually enacted in the transference-countertransference matrix. When engaged and perceived there is a release of relational constrictions that have come from the past so that both participants experience new "relational freedom" (1997, 2002, in press). This mutual therapeutic work is so emotionally intense, draining, and time-consuming that effective treatment can be expected to span several years—optimally at more than once a week often with periods of telephone contact in between. This is not only a widespread clinical finding, but the empirical research supporting the *PDM* makes clear that successful psychodynamic therapy necessarily spans a number of years.

The strain on the therapist involves:

(1) holding steady sometimes for lengthy periods,
(2) building trust by empathically responding to the content offered, and
(3) commenting regularly on the actual relational engagements and disengagements in the therapy setting until the client gets the gist of what their relatedness issues are and what their relatedness patterns are costing them.
(4) Then comes the struggle. Like a good parent encouraging a frightened child to walk or ride a bicycle or to engage in some other daunting task, the therapist must stand by and firmly insist on moving forward into new and breathtaking relational ventures—despite the overwhelming fear, fragmentation, and physical agony necessarily involved.

Typically we see a long period or a series of periods in which the client experiences discouragement, depression, dysfunction, and deadening fragmentation and fear before she/he can be coaxed into trying new relational modes. Therapeutic victory only slowly dawns— but not without numerous demoralizing collapses and setbacks on the part of the client with frequent periods of frustration and despair on the part of the therapist. This process is what we will look at from several different angles. First let's think about what's actually involved in "the psychotherapy relationship".

The History of the Psychotherapeutic Relationship

Over the century since Sigmund Freud first invented psychotherapy or "the talking cure," many helpful ideas and practices have emerged. Psychotherapy started as a medical science partly because Freud was a physician and partly because the scientific paradigm of objectifying things was in its heyday and the human mind was viewed as another thing to be scientifically investigated. In his early studies of hypnosis with Charcot in 1885 Freud first grasped that many physical symptoms had an unconscious psychological origin and could be relieved through psychological interventions. But it was not until he listened to his colleague Wilhelm Fleiss discuss the startling case of Anna O. (Bertha Pappenheim), who had developed a false pregnancy in the course of her treatment, that Freud first understood the power of the unconscious.

> From manifestations in their relationship Freud intuited the important connection between unconscious fantasies and psychically determined physical manifestations....Moreover, Freud understood that highly personal unconscious influences in both doctor and patient could be mobilized and laid bare for observation under the influence of an intense personal relationship." (Hedges, 1992, p. 41)

Descriptive psychiatry, however, has historically remained allied to a medical model searching for the cause, course, and cure of mental diseases. The evolution of this medically oriented approach is well documented in a succession of Diagnostic and Statistic Manuals of the American Psychiatric Association. In the many *DSM* revisions proliferating pathologies continue to be generated and abstracted along with presumed causes, treatment, and cures. But worse than pathologizing unnecessarily and being merely descriptive, the *DSM* is relationally barren. No real person with all of her eccentricities is depicted as in any real way interacting with any other real person with all of his eccentricities. That is, there is no real sense of how the depicted traits or behaviors might have evolved in the context of real relationships or might have an opportunity to be understood or transformed through real therapeutic relationships. It's as if descriptive psychiatry knows nothing about our relational origin and nothing about our relational destiny and how it can be enriched and transformed through intimate relating.

"What's wrong with you and how can I fix you?" is the central medical question that has been mistakenly imported into the field of psychotherapy. The same question, "What's wrong with you and how can I fix you?", echoes the worst of all messages we received from our parents, teachers, and caregivers during the course of growing up. From a psychological standpoint, "What's wrong with you and how can I fix you?" is hardly a decent way to relate to any human being because it immediately sets up a non-mutual, non-equal "one-up, one-down" relational situation whose implicit aim is to establish superiority and control over and perhaps even to shame and humiliate the other into submission or compliance. So while determining "what's wrong with you" may be relevant to the practice of medicine, it's certainly not helpful to the practice of psychotherapy. We understand that many physical symptoms result from psychological stress and trauma, but the "what's wrong with you" question serves to focus on the physical or mental symptom, not on the underlying relational templates that have given rise to that symptom. Additionally, for a client to be encouraged to ask, "what's wrong with me" puts that person immediately into a place of insecurity, shame, fear, and "one-down," usually with an accompanying sense of incompetency, and/or self-loathing—not at all helpful attitudes in the psychotherapeutic inquiry. In order to address early-learned relational modes, psychotherapy must be understood first and foremost as a relational practice that aims for expanded mutual understanding (consciousness) of ourselves and the ways we habitually relate to others—not a fixing or curing of anything.

In addition to theories of pathology, we have inherited theories of personality, theories of human development, and theories of how people change. Implicit in all of these theories is a positivist belief of "how things really are, how the mind really works." But in human life and in therapy, we know there are no clear truths to be found, rather many ever-changing truths to be spoken and listened to.

In the more than a century since psychotherapy began many brilliant clinicians have attempted to articulate in diverse ways what to them constitutes psychotherapy. Running throughout the history of our theoretical and clinical work is a recognition of the importance of the relationship between the client and therapist and how each experiences the other. But only with recent neuropsychological and psychotherapy research has it become clear that the centerpiece of psychotherapy *is the actual therapeutic relationship itself.* This singular finding changes forever how we conceptualize therapy and what we understand to be important in therapy—regardless of how each practitioner chooses to practice. That is, if what is finally decisive in human development and life is emotional relatedness then how do we form theories that help us listen for each person's relationship experiences on a moment-to-moment basis? In my writings I have emphasized the need for theoretical approaches that aim not to tell us how this person's mind or life really is, but rather theories that provide Listening Perspectives on the idiosyncratic ways each person experiences the world, themselves, and their relationships.

It's not that our accumulated wisdom gathered in a positivist truth mode is misguided because it isn't. Rather, the relational aspect—engagement and disengagement—explicit and implicit in all therapies now takes center stage. Having understood at last the centrality of the relationship in psychotherapy—no matter what one's personal clinical orientation—let us move to considering the wide range of human relatedness potentials that we might listen for during clinical hours.

Developmental-Relational Listening

Over the last century four distinctly different Listening Perspectives in psychotherapy have evolved for listening and responding to the unique relatedness qualities that each person lives out on a daily basis (see Hedges 1983, 2005). These Listening Perspectives are essentially metaphors derived from observing relationship developments in early childhood. Four relatedness levels or perspectives is an arbitrary number based on logical considerations of self-and-other relationship possibilities. That is, from a developmental standpoint we can say that the simplest relatedness modes are those that developed in early life, while the more complex ones require considerably more relational experience and learning. So we might say that borderline, bipolar, schizophrenic, psychotic, and characterological relatedness modes that developed early in life and the relational fears associated with them are relatively simple. For different listening purposes different perspectives are needed. For example, when considering relational desires and fears that develop along the way it is convenient to consider seven relational fears. The four Listening Perspectives organized on an axis of increasing complexity and seven accompanying relational fears are listed in Table 1. In Appendix D a more comprehensive table of Developmental Relational Listening is included.

**Table 1: Four Developmental Listening Perspectives
and Seven Relational Fears**

I. The Organizing experience

  1. The fear of being alone

  2. The fear of making connections

II. The Symbiotic experience

  3. The fear of abandonment

  4. The fear of self-assertion

III. The self-other experience

  5. The fear of being unacceptable

IV. The independent experience

  6. The fear of failure and success

  7. The fear of being fully alive

A person could experience focal or cumulative trauma in relationships at any stage of life and need to re-experience that trauma in a therapeutic relationship in order to work through the post-traumatic experiences that are still creating problems. But truly terrifying and deeply traumatic experiences that impact the fundamental ways the personality organizes itself are more characteristic of the earliest stages of development—the Organizing and the Symbiotic experiences. Anyone subjected to overwhelming terror, intimidation, or shame during one of the earliest phases of life is vulnerable to having similar overwhelming levels of fear, constriction, and/or fragmentation triggered by intimate relationships later in life.

Let me now elaborate the four Listening Perspectives (Hedges 1983, 2005) and the seven associated relational fears (Hedges 2012a,

2013a). For our present purposes in this book we will only be interested in the Organizing and Symbiotic experiences.

I. THE ORGANIZING EXPERIENCE: Infants require certain forms of connection and inter-connection in order to remain psychologically alert and enlivened to themselves and to others. In their early relatedness they are busy "Organizing" physical and mental channels of connection—first to mother's body, later to her mind and to the minds of others—for nurturance, stimulation, soothing, and evacuation. Framing Organizing patterns for analysis entails studying how two people approach to make connections and then turn away, veer off, rupture, or dissipate the intensity of the connections

    1. The Fear of Being Alone: We dread reaching out and finding nobody there to respond to our needs. We fear being ignored, being left alone, and being seen as unimportant. We feel the world does not respond to our needs. So what's the use of trying?

    2. The Fear of Interpersonally Connecting: Because of frightening and painful experiences in the past, connecting emotionally and intimately with others feels dangerous. Our life experiences have left us feeling that the world is not a safe place. We fear injury so we avoid and withdraw from connections.

II. THE SYMBIOTIC EXPERIENCE: Toddlers are busy learning how to make emotional relationships (both good and bad) work for them. They experience a sense of merger and reciprocity with their primary caregivers, thus establishing many knee-jerk, automatic, characterological, and role-reversible patterns or scenarios of relatedness. Framing the symbiotic relatedness patterns for analysis entails noting how each person characteristically engages the other and how interactive scenarios evolve from two subjectively-formed sets of internalized self-and-other interaction patterns.

3. The Fear of Being Abandoned: After having connected emotionally or bonded with someone, we fear being either abandoned with our own needs or being swallowed up by the other person's needs. In either case, we feel the world is not a dependable place and that we live in danger of emotional abandonment. We may become clingy and dependent, or we may become super independent—or both.

4. The Fear of Self-Assertion: We have all experienced rejection, and perhaps even punishment for expressing ourselves in a way that others don't like. We thus may learn to fear asserting ourselves and letting our needs be known in relationships. We feel the world does not allow us to be truly ourselves. We may either cease putting ourselves out there altogether, or we may assert ourselves with demanding vengeance.

III. THE SELF-OTHER EXPERIENCE: Two- and-three-year-olds are preoccupied with using the acceptance and approval of others for developing and enhancing self definitions, self skills, and self-esteem. Their relatedness strivings use the mirroring, twinning, and idealizing responses of significant others to firm up their budding sense of self. Framing for analysis the self-other patterns used for affirming, confirming, and inspiring the self entails studying how the internalized mirroring, twinning, and idealizing patterns used in self development in the pasts of both participants play out to enhance and limit the possibilities for mutual self-to-self-other resonance in the emerging interpersonal engagement.

5. The Fear of Lack of Recognition: When we do not get the acceptance and confirmation we need in relationships, we are left with a feeling of not being seen or recognized for whom we really are. Or, we may fear that others will only respect and love us if we are who they want us to be. We may work continuously to feel seen and recognized by others, or we may give up in rage, humiliation, or shame.

IV. THE INDEPENDENCE EXPERIENCE: Four- to-seven-year-olds are dealing with triangular love and hate relationships and are moving toward more complex social relationships. In their relatedness they experience others as separate centers of initiative and themselves as independent agents in a socially competitive environment. Framing the internalized patterns of independently-interacting selves in both cooperative and competitive triangulations with real and fantasized third parties entails studying the emerging interaction patterns for evidence of repressive forces operating within each participant and between the analytic couple that work to limit or spoil the full interactive potential.

6. The Fear of Failure and Success: When we have loved and lost or tried and failed, we may fear painful competitive experiences. When we have succeeded or won—possibly at someone else's expense—we may experience guilt or fear retaliation. Thus, we learn to hold back in love and life, thereby not risking either failure or success. We may feel the world does not allow us to be fulfilled. Or we may feel guilty and afraid for feeling fulfilled.

7. The Fear of Being Fully Alive: Our expansiveness, creative energy, and joy in our aliveness inevitably come into conflict with family, work, religion, and society. We come to believe that we must curtail our aliveness to conform to the expectations and demands of the world. We feel the world does not permit us to be fully, joyfully, and passionately alive. Rather than putting our whole selves out there with full energy, we may throw in the towel, succumb to mediocre conformity, or fall into living deadness.

Two Relational Intervention Principles

Based on the above sketch of relatedness-potential going from simpler to more complex, it might appear as if I am offering a developmental theory of relatedness rather than articulating a series of metaphors that can serve as Listening Perspectives during the course of psychotherapy. I am absolutely not! That's the old-fashioned medicalized way of considering patients with illnesses that the well doctor is going to fix. That's the positivist way of approaching science with an observed object and an observing subject. That's the modernist way of viewing truth as something that can be finally discovered and known. As psychotherapists we have come too far to allow ourselves these outmoded ways of thinking and being. We live now in the age of consciousness-raising, of subjectivity and intersubjectivity, of post-modernism where realities are socially constructed and ever changing. This means that we are forever in a soup of uncertainty struggling to construct ways of perceiving that move us along toward new possibilities! In therapy this means constructing Listening Perspectives—points of view we can momentarily assume to help us grasp what is happening in the moment between us and our clients. Pat theories and techniques are for the faint-hearted! We must be ready to shift on a moment's notice. This means that our own relational histories that have left us with constrictions in thought and affect are at all times engaged with our clients and that we are, therefore, in for constant surprises about ourselves. I have dealt in detail with all four developmentally-based Listening Perspectives in a series of books (Hedges 1983, 1992, 1994a,b,c,1996, 2000b, 2012a, 2013a) but in the present book I refocus my earlier thinking on the earliest two Listening Perspectives and the four relational fears associated with them.

The earliest four relational fear experiences or what elsewhere I have called fear-reflexes (Hedges 2012a, 2013a), in addition to being universal, are more basic and less complex than later learned relational modes and relational fears. When carefully approached and understood, a therapist can develop an ease and even an enjoyment in being with early forms and aspects of personality organization. But, unfortunately, many therapists so easily become confused and overwhelmed with content or their own dissociations that they fail to attend to the relational processes involved in treating developmentally early experiences. As corollary, all people have experienced these earlier relational modes in the course of development and have created relational solutions to the dilemmas they experienced during their own early levels of development. Therefore, even people capable of highly complex relatedness modes have "pockets" of borderline or psychotic experience that can be triggered in certain kinds of stressful relational situations and that may need to be therapeutically explored. For us therapists this point is particularly cogent because the nature of our work brings us into contact with all manner of emotional stresses that we cannot afford to be overly defensive about if we are to be effective therapists. Said differently, *the intense relational demands that we therapists face on a daily basis make it essential that in our own therapy and ongoing personal and professional development we develop as much relational freedom as possible—and that includes the freedom to be stuck, confused, defeated, and despairing in our work.*

The two relational intervention principles I will elaborate in this book are based on *engagement and disengagement*:

1. When therapeutically responding to bipolar, schizophrenic, and other psychotic organizations (Listening Perspective I) there is a need to study the person's approaches to engagements and then to intervene in affective or cognitive disengagements—in whatever ways possible.
2. When responding therapeutically to borderline and character personality organizations (Listening Perspective II) a full affective replication (enactment) of symbiotic (dyadic) relational experience is required before the scenarios can be perceived, reacted to, confronted, and relinquished.

A frequently made error is for the therapist to be seduced into thinking some more complex relatedness interaction is occurring when actually some form of early Symbiotic engagement or Organizing disengagement is occurring.

Summarizing, Part I of this book has been devoted to considering the relational nature of human beings and how this relational nature has been bypassed by traditional systems of diagnostic thinking and content-oriented theories of therapy. Two principles of relational intervention are noted: engagement and disengagement. I have suggested that listening to engagement and disengagement processes as they occur on a moment-to-moment basis in therapy can best be accomplished by considering developmental levels of relatedness-complexity along with developmentally-based relational fears.

Part II of this book will consider the Organizing experience and how the first principle of engagement and disengagement can lead to effective Relational Interventions.

Part III of this book will consider the Symbiotic experience and how the second principle of replicated or enacted engagement and disengagement can lead to effective Relational Interventions. The expected outcome of Relational Interventions is greater flexibility in relatedness potentials or, in Donnel Stern's words, greater "relational freedom".

In Part IV I conclude by discussing the therapeutic importance of distinguishing between relational moments that stem from the Organizing experience and ones that stem from the Symbiotic experience because in practice the distinction is not always so clear— nor should it be since, after all, Symbiotic experience is built upon relational templates first set up in the Organizing experience.

Part II

Identifying and Engaging the Organizing Transference

Identifying transference experiences from the earliest level of development begins with the assumption that if psychological attachment—the bonding or symbiotic dance—has not occurred or has only partially occurred, there is a reason. That is, extensive attachment research among mammals makes clear that biological attachment is a fundamental genetically-determined drive mechanism (Fonagy, et. al 2002). In the human species a well-known set of psychological attachment styles predictably follow. So when, for whatever the reason, psychological attachment has not or has only partially or faultily occurred we can surmise that some sort of irregularity arose in the earliest months of life to restrict expectable interpersonal engagements. Closed-off psychic channels for human connection and somatic constrictions that make physical extensions painful are retained in the personality and in the body structure in ways that can be observed in later life as the Organizing (or psychotic) transference. This earliest of transferences represents or expresses learning experiences of the infant that occurred whenever he or she emotionally extended or reached out and was somehow turned away, not met, or negatively greeted. The questing activity was met with environmental response that taught the infant not to strive in that way again. The "never go there again" lesson effectively marks infant attempts to organize experience—marks that can later be identified as transference in the therapeutic relationship. With people living Organizing experiences, the transference structure can be seen as systematically functioning to limit the achievement of or to prevent the maintenance of sustained human emotional contact. That is, the person learned as an infant that emotional contact is dangerous, frightening, traumatic, and/or life threatening. Relatedness learning during the earliest months of life becomes organized around limiting the extension or reaching-out experience and preventing all potential forms of contact felt to be frightening, unsatisfying, or unsafe. Framing the Organizing transference involves studying how two people approach to make connections and then turn away, veer off, rupture, or dissipate the intensity of the connections. *It goes without saying that unless the treatment situation is successful in stimulating a desire to connect and encouraging successive attempts at connecting, we cannot hope to study the ways that connection is avoided or the disconnect is accomplished.*

Three Brief Case Examples of Fight-Flight-Freeze Predefenses

Three case examples highlighting what Selma Fraiberg (1982) has called fight-flight-freeze predefenses—primordial ways of avoiding connections—will illustrate how an Organizing experience can appear and how we as therapists can gain some grasp of the meaning of the Organizing transference experience.

1. Fight in the Organizing Transference

The first case example is from a female therapist who has been treating a woman twice a week for three years. An intense therapeutic relationship has developed. The client is a very bright and

28

sophisticated professional. She lives very comfortably in the everyday world but suffers privately from what she refers to as a "multiple personality." The most troubling switch is when, without apparent reason, she goes into a rageful self. Her therapist sought a crisis consultation after she got this telephone call after their last session: "I'm not coming in anymore because there's something wrong with our relationship." The therapist inquired about the nature of the problem. The patient replied, "I can tell you feel there's something wrong with my relationship with Naomi." Naomi is a lesbian with whom the patient has developed an intimate relationship. She continued, "You don't think that it's right, or you think there's something wrong with Naomi. There's no point in our going any further so long as you think that way." She was angry, shouting at her therapist, and then she listed a number of other things, "You don't listen this way … and you're not that way …"—a tirade of complaints and accusations.

Her therapist is in a state of shock, feeling she may never see her client again. She is not even clear about what might have been said to upset her. She tells the consultant that her client is basically not lesbian: she had three or four relationships with women, but ones in which she was looking for soothing contact with a woman, possibly in order to feel mothered. She cannot develop relationships with men because she does not know how to relate to men. She is confused and frightened by men. She has said various times that, even though she is having a sexual relationship with a woman, she does not feel she is lesbian—she does not feel like other lesbians. The client feels certain she is really not a lesbian. At one point the therapist had said, "I really don't think you're a lesbian, either."

I have reported extensively elsewhere (1994c) on this case and the two that follow, but for present purposes we can see that the reflective comment the therapist made about her not really being a lesbian is used by the client in order to accomplish a rageful disconnect. The therapist reviewed the misunderstanding and learned from the episode that rage becomes the way of accomplishing relationship ruptures when intimacy of certain types threatens. Of special interest here is a screen memory in which the patient, who grew up in poverty conditions, witnessed her mother have an abortion and flush the fetus down the toilet. The mother's rage at having needy children appears to have been one of the sources of the rageful disconnecting mechanism. In the counter-transference, the therapist was able to report the passing fantasy of letting the patient go because she promised to be so difficult.

This episode represents the patient's first tentative foray into working the Organizing transference directly with her therapist, though a series of parallel transferences with friends had been discussed extensively. Now the therapist has a clearer view of the nature of the disconnecting transference replication. The Organizing transference typically is worked through in a series of waves or episodes. The therapist will be more prepared to act quickly next time to deal with the disconnecting intent. The interpretation may be accomplished in the nonverbal or preverbal way; the therapist stays with her in her rageful self and invites her to stay connected and to live out her terror of being with the therapist together rather than to disconnect or rupture the connection with rage.

2. Flight in the Organizing Transference

The second example of Organizing transference involves a female therapist who has been seeing a client for three or four years. This client has been driving an hour and a half each week to her appointment ("So there's a long umbilicus," the therapist says). The client has presented as tenuous in her ability to maintain relationships. In the last six months she has talked frequently about terminating therapy because of money and distance. She canceled her sessions in bad weather and during the winter holiday rush. On several occasions the therapist has empathically tried the following, "Well, okay, I can understand how busy you are and how far it is. You have accomplished a number of things in therapy, so if you want to consider termination, we can talk about that." She has even suggested helping the patient find a therapist who was geographically closer. But that all became taboo. The client was allowed to talk about termination, but the therapist was forbidden to talk about it.

On the occasion in question, the client called during the Christmas holidays and, without any warning, canceled all future appointments. Her therapist made several phone calls to contact her. She sent a Christmas card. She did everything she could to reach out to her. The therapist thought, "Well, maybe it's best that she stop—and this is her way of stopping. Maybe I shouldn't pursue her." In my view this laissez-faire attitude may be appropriate for listening to more differentiated forms of personality organization but is clearly not empathic when working an Organizing transference in which the client cannot initiate or sustain connection and is frequently compelled to break it through some form of flight. The therapist is an empathic and intuitive woman who remained persistent in her attempts to restore the connection. They finally did connect by phone, and the therapist discovered what happened. The client said, "In the last session I was telling you about my friend Valerie, and you turned away. Then I knew you didn't care for me, so there wasn't any point in coming back."

The consultant says, "She's found a way to live out the Organizing transference of mother disconnecting and used the Valerie content to accomplish it. This is the window to the Organizing experience we are waiting for. We patiently wait for the moment in which the reenactment of the turning away, the breaking of contact, the rupture of experience happens in the transference." As the case was reviewed, therapist and consultant located a number of such breaches in which the client needed to flee the developing intimacy of the relationship.

The therapist was fired up with these ideas because they seemed to make sense and to organize in her mind many past incidents. She is ready to talk to her client about all this right away. The consultant cautioned her not to rush into verbal interpretations about something that is perennially lived out nonverbally. The therapist tunes in quickly and says, "I feel like where we're at right now is both lying down in a playpen, and I have to wait for her to come to me." The consultant reminded her that the baby has to be allowed to find the breast, but it must be available to be found—not somewhere in flight and not through talk. The transference to the psychotic mother will be reenacted again and again, so there will be ample time to discuss what is happening. But the therapist can use her new understanding to simply be with her client in new ways. She was reminded of what she already knew from her studies of the Organizing experience: that abstract verbal interpretations *per se* will not touch this very early transference.

Interpretation at the Organizing level must be a concrete activity, often manifest in some token physical gesture, interpretive contact, or touch at the specific moment when the analytic client is actually in the act of pulling away from contact, of (transferentially) creating a rupture. Viable interpretation of the Organizing transference often involves some form of actual, physical, concrete reaching out by one person toward another to communicate, "I know you believe you must break off our personal engagement in this way now. But it is not true. As an adult, you have the ability to stay here now with me and to experience your long-standing terror of connectedness. How can you manage not to leave me now? Can we find a way to remain in contact for just a few more minutes?"[1] Clients needing to work on Organizing experience terror often deliberately (and perhaps wisely) conduct the early phases of therapy at quite some distance from the therapist by spacing appointments far apart or arranging long and difficult drives. They often sit at a distance from the therapist and talk about seemingly unrelated things. They know that interpersonal closeness can only be experienced as traumatic. Thus, the invitation to sustain contact must be cautiously offered and episodes of flight anticipated and responded to appropriately.

3. Freezing in the Organizing Transference

In the third example of how Organizing transference works, an emerging theme of an otherwise very-well-developed woman has been related to the Organizing period. This example is from a much later working-through period of the analysis (with a male therapist) and occurs in a personality much more capable of verbal abstractions than the previous two. The woman's mother, during the baby's early months of life, was afraid to pick her up for fear of "breaking" her. The client actually believes she can recall her mother frequently lurking or hovering just out of sight so she would not beg to be picked up. In transference she would often lie on the couch absolutely motionless for long periods listening to the quiet sounds of the analyst breathing, clearing his throat, or stirring in his chair. It has been discovered through several years of intensive psychotherapy that there were many strengths this mother was able to stimulate in this child, but at the deepest psychic level there remain connecting difficulties. The emergent theme over several weeks to be reported was the analytic client's rage that occurs on a fairly regular basis in social situations when she knows that the person she's interacting with can indeed do more for her and be more there for her, but somehow flakes out. In short, her rage is mobilized at people when they have potentially more to offer than in fact the person is actively living in the current relationship.

In a key session she develops the theme further. Early in the marriage, she says, her husband was far more warm, giving, and available than he is now, and she is angry that he is not more available when she knows he can be. She becomes exasperated to the point of feeling *utterly helpless and frozen.* By the same token, she indicates that what attracted her to a close friend was that this other woman had so much to give. The friend is well-traveled and well-read. She is alive, active, versatile, a good conversationalist, and much more. But, in a recent example, when her friend had the flu and could not get out of bed to go to her son's very first baseball game: "Then I don't see her any longer as what she could be or might be for me if she can't [even] be there for her own son. I become angry and disillusioned with her and withdraw into myself. Now I know what has been bothering me so much lately about her in our relationship: too often she cancels, flakes out, or blobs out when I know she doesn't have to, when I know she has far more to give but is choosing not to. I become completely *immobilized, frozen*, in impotent rage."

In the discussion of various examples that have occurred with her husband and her friend, she said, "Now I'm finding that not only when I'm enraged at the other person for not living up to their potential do I not get what they have to offer me, but I also see that when I'm enraged I am totally unable to take in, to get, to make use of that which they can in fact offer me." She referenced some examples from previous transference experiences in therapy in which she, in complaining bitterly about the therapist's seemingly endless unavailability over the holidays and weekends, was so preoccupied in her hours leading up to the holidays that she was unable to make use of whatever good experiences might be possible in the sessions. Her comment is "Something always happens." The emphasis here is on the subjective statement of the disconnecting experience being impersonal. It's not "I'm disappointed with the other" or "The other lets me down" or "The other fails to live up to his potential." It's "We're interacting, and then something happens, and the potential that is there isn't being lived out, and I fall into a lost state of sadness and grief, which is usually manifest in instantaneous but frozen rage."

At this point in the session the client realizes she has lost or repressed a further insight regarding her husband and friend that she was very excited about only a moment before when she connected to it. But just as quickly as the insight came, it fled and she was very disturbed for some time about having lost this insight. After a few thoughtful moments, she said, "It sounds like a reason to break contact." The therapist quickly replied, "No, it's the *way* you break contact." The client then said excitedly, "That's exactly what I lost. I was trying to formulate the problem with my husband and my friend in terms of how I break contact, but I couldn't quite get there. If I'm always living in what a person could give me but isn't, then several things happen: One, I have reason not to relate to them; two, I'm not relating to them at all but I'm relating rather to my fantasy; and three, they do have something to give or I wouldn't be relating to them, but in my distress and frozen anger I'm completely missing what they have to give to me. I break the contact by being sad and enraged, complaining about what I'm not getting."

At this point she slowed down and indicated that she was emoting very deeply, that she felt she'd reached a very profound point. "I know somehow that this can change my life if I can finally get hold of it. If I can find some way of fully knowing about this, I will be able to change many things." Her therapist said, "It seems as though you have located the mechanism regarding how the contact is broken and how it relates to the early experiences of your mother who, much of the time, was there so that you knew full well what things she could provide. But when she was preoccupied, or not willing or able to give, or frightened about how she might harm you, she bowed out, leaving you stuck, knowing that she could give more but that she was not giving it. No wonder she reports that you were such a good baby and slept a lot! The content of the transference is 'You could be giving me more, but you're not.'"

"Now," she continued, "I find I'm a little scared about knowing all this. Things keep clicking in my mind—more and more examples. It's like my whole life is built on this single mechanism. No wonder I wasn't happy when John, my supervisor, failed to tune in to me completely when I knew he could. If I finally identify this, I may be able to change. I am excited, but I think I'm mostly very scared. I think the scare is that I won't remember this, I won't be able to take hold of it, I won't be able to make it my own." The therapist said, "No, the scare is that you *will* remember it. You are in the process of deep change, and as you are changing you are coming face to face with a terror you have avoided all your life. The terror of having to encounter a real live person who has some good things to offer but who may not, for a variety of reasons, be willing or able to give fully in all areas. Sooner or later in every relationship you encounter this situation, and it brings back the agonizingly sad and rageful reactions you had to your mother during your earliest months of life. So you have been unable to continue relating or you have given up the relating when the conditions are not met rightly. What you are scared of is actually allowing yourself to negotiate the uncertainties of relationships and to survive the positive possibilities as well as the painful disappointments which are bound to be a frightening and powerful consequence of fully knowing and living out what you are now discovering."

"I know you're right," she says.

Each of these three examples illustrates how the rupture of the Organizing experience is repeated in transference. In each instance, multiple interpretive possibilities exist. The decisive moment of Organizing transference interpretation is not visible in any of these examples—in the first two because the relationship had not yet arrived there, and in the third because the in vivo interpretations had already begun and the client was in a later stage of "owning" the interpretative work (though she expresses fear of losing it). The presence of Fraiberg's (1982) three "predefenses" of fighting, fleeing, and freezing is suggested in these three case vignettes and may be seen as the clients' ways of achieving a rupture of contact in the relationship that, due to transference projections, is threatening to become overstimulating.

Disconnecting Modes: "The Clamor"

Psychotherapy with Organizing level transference is full of all kinds of content and behavior, even if that content should take the form of extreme belligerence, withdrawal or silence. Over the years I have come to stigmatize various disengagement modes emanating from the content of the Organizing transference as "the clamor of the therapy hour." To me, clamor implies two things: First, clamor is an incessant cry or demand for more, for special consideration, for "what I need and have a right to now—before I fragment or die." But secondly, clamor is a cry that is so intense and so intrusive as to be annoying, alienating, and contact-rupturing. Undoubtedly the original function of the cry was to signal distress and to demand that the mothering partner restore a body-mind-relationship state that could be enjoyed or tolerated. But when the cry becomes a conditioned part of an infant's life that cannot be adequately calmed, it becomes a conditioned response to any perturbation. Subsequently the clamor is systematically paired with or conditioned to a sense of the presence of the (m)other who is failing to relieve the perturbation or pain. So through simple conditioning, trust relationships later become the object of terror, in proportion to whatever extent they were originally unsuccessful in quelling the rising tide of overwhelming distress and pain. Later trust relationships are then imbued with this conditioned fear and its accompanying clamor. The clamor thus comes to serve as an alienating wedge between people to prevent the danger of intimate relating. "Clamorous" content or behavior thus becomes a conditioned method of averting the challenge necessarily posed by interpersonal engagements.

Clamor takes myriad forms. But in therapy it functions to produce a breach in interpersonal connection or to limit the possibility of satisfying and sustained connection. Therapists with good training in empathy try in the therapeutic process to ride out the cry, to empathize with the need—the demand associated with the clamor—and with the frustration that needs are not being adequately met. Unfortunately, empathy with the content of the clamor often serves to escalate its intensity, delay its punch, and reinforce its alienating function. What is not being realized by limited content-based empathy is that the content of the clamor cannot be satisfied because, *as cry, it is a memory with a purpose* but not necessarily a relevant content. *The purpose is to prevent or forestall empathic contact which is perceived as dangerous.* The clamor is an angry memory of what I needed and didn't get. But the conditioned clamor-memory now functions in the service of preventing intimate or reciprocal interconnections that in the past were known to be traumatic. What is remembered is the pain of a previous relation or connection that was experienced as dangerous or terrifying. Either total muscular collapse or muscle system constriction that functions to withdraw from, ward off, or quell the pain then provides its own form of permanently conditioned pain response—which, over a lifetime, the person comes to fear. Successful relational therapy eventually involves re-experiencing the agonizing body-mind-relationship pain and releasing it.

In summary, *the trust relationship itself mobilizes conditioned physical-psychological pain responses.* The cry or clamor serves to ward off present and future connections by alienating the other and creating a safety zone to prevent anticipated re-occurring relationship trauma. Once an expression of pain in relationship, the clamorous cry now functions as a defense against relationship re-traumatization through foreclosing meaningful emotional connections. Since emotional connections, mutual affect regulation experiences, are necessary prerequisites for learning the many lessons of life, the person's growth remains severely limited. The person is terrified of connections, of relationship, because interconnectedness in the primordial past was known to be hurtful. To connect in the present is to run the risk of stimulating pain again. There are many ways to prevent relatedness— one is a clamorous cry for "more," for "what I deserve," for how "you're not treating me right," or how "you're not giving me what I need," or for how "I can find somebody better who will." "Abandonment!" in one form or another can be another clamorous or accusatory cry. But with Organizing level relatedness it is essentially bogus because it is used not to promote or to restore relating as it might be in a symbiotic relatedness mode. Rather, the clamorous abandonment cry serves to forestall or to prevent connection or to create a break in connections! Virtually all "psychotic symptoms" serve the purpose of clamor, of keeping others safely at bay.

Brief Case Illustrations of How Clamor Works in the Organizing Transference

One man who was born with a birth defect that prevented sucking sought older women prostitutes and then complained that he couldn't orgasm with them. Soothing sensual contact was what had been missing, and when he now goes for it he does it in ways that are self-limiting, he then focuses on his sexual dysfunction rather than on his self-frustrated yearning for closeness and his terror of relationship. "It's their fault. They don't satisfy me."

A woman client who had been mechanically managed by her mother out of a sense of obligation and duty in infancy, begged her therapist for physical touch because she was internally prevented from feeling his mental presence and touch. He knew that the soothing physical touch that she longed for was available to her in many ways in her life but that it didn't relieve her internalized agony over lack of touch from him. Her clamor for physical touch from him not only kept him uneasy and distant in the relationship, but prevented the very mental and emotional closeness and soothing that would allow her to participate in transformational relating.

Another man maintains a schizoid or bored demeanor in relationships until the other almost forcibly approaches him with overriding, warm, affirming interest. He thinks he is afraid to approach others because he might be rejected, but in fact his manner staves off the possibility of connection that he is terrified of. When there are brief moments of personal connection with his therapist he suffers terrifying nightmares and phobias. He remains stuck in the belief that others "don't relate well, don't approach me right."

Numerous such therapy relations end with the client bitterly complaining about the shortcomings of the therapist. Yet when the interaction is closely scrutinized we can see that the clamor and accusatory cries only serve to justify the client's retreat, and that there was an unwillingness or inability to continue negotiating the relating. Somehow the therapeutic relationship had not developed the interpersonal safety needed for two to work through the terrors of connectedness together. The plea is always somehow "Don't abandon me, I need you." But the plea comes in the form of a clamor bound to alienate and replicate the original abandonment.

Suicidal and other self-destructive and self-effacing behaviors usually serve the same alienating purposes. The clamor stems not from abandonment fear, as the client is inclined to claim, but from the terror of meaningful connections. The memory expressed in this way is the danger of connecting, the terror of a deeply personal I-thou exchange that has the power to transform. The content of the clamor invariably revolves around some charge—aimed at the therapist or at others—of rejection, neglect, abandonment, misunderstanding, or abuse. The therapist is thrown some tantalizing bone to chew on which serves as resistance to the two experiencing the full impact of the terrifying transference—thus derailing the therapeutic process. The content is designed to fend off intimate and meaningful relating. The content is designed to take the focus away from the mutually enacted disengagement from intimate connection.

A Thought Experiment for Understanding the Organizing experience

Imagine yourself approaching someone with whom you are in the process of developing or expanding an emotionally significant relationship. Your companion likewise approaches. It could be your spouse, your child, one of your parents, a sibling or a friend, or even someone special with whom you work or play. Perhaps it is one of your clients if you are a therapist. Perhaps your therapist if you are a client.

You feel alive and happy to be seeing your special person and excited by all that is mutual in the approach. There is a smile on both faces and warm greetings in both voices. Both sets of eyes gleam with eager anticipation. Two hearts pick up their pace as the relating dance begins. You two have been in this pace many times before, co-creating experiences of joy, laughter, sadness, grief, anger, inspiration, mutual regard, and love.

Actually try right now to conjure up in your mind such a relational situation. Put the book down for a moment, close your eyes, look at your relating partner with your mind's eye, feel the approach and the anticipation, and imagine something wonderful starting to happen between you. As the relating dance begins, each makes her or his own move, and each mutually responds, reciprocating with an expanding resonance leading to the creation of intense harmonies and cacophonies of sound, sight, shadow, color, texture, stillness, excitement, life, and movement.

But then, almost before your realize it, just when things are starting to get good, the intensity of the relating game somehow starts to diminish. You begin feeling something happening in your body, in your mind, in your soul. Your sixth sense has a hold on you and is slowing you down somehow, pulling you back, inexplicably dampening the intensity of the momentarily achieved and longed-for connection. Perhaps you are thinking of how many things you have to do today. Or some part of you is drifting off toward unrelated thoughts and pictures. In your reverie you mind find yourself feeling drowsy, moody, tired, or cautious for no reason you can really think of.

You make a quick, valiant attempt as the relating dance continues to figure out what's going on with you, or what's going on with your partner in the interaction. You wonder what's happening in your bodies and in the relationship at the moment that's causing this slowing, this distancing, this breach in the intimate contact.

As therapists we have some skill at the relating game so you may attempt processing with our relating partner the physical and mental impingements that have just cropped up for you. "Why am I so uncomfortable or distracted or feeling this way at this particular moment?" Perhaps you feel edgy, nervous, hypersensitive, distracted or constricted. Perhaps you find yourself losing interest, slumping, or rapidly dropping in energy level. An invisible wall has gone up. Emotional distance is threatening. "What's happening around here, anyway? This is the child I love so deeply. These moments are fleeting and precious, why am I feeling bored? This is my spouse, my love with whom I would rather spend time with than anyone else on earth, so why am I mentally fleeing the scene. This is my friend, my trusted colleague, my valued client or my therapist with whom I truly treasure my time, so what's happening to spoil my enjoyment, to wreck these few precious moments of intimacy, to limit my opportunity for enrichment and transformation?"

You attempt a quick recovery. Maybe you are able to take a deep breath and dive back into the rapid-paced fray of the relating dance and be okay. Maybe not. Perhaps the processing has helped momentarily. Maybe you suspect that the particular trend towards disconnection that you are experiencing at this moment haunts the bigger picture of your relationships, your intimacy, your love. And this does so in subtle or perhaps not so subtle ways for a lifetime.

"How does what I am experiencing now fit with the bigger picture of my life? What are my hopes and desire here? What are my dreads and fears?" You may even go so far as to ask yourself, "What's the matter with me? What's my problem? What do I do this so much—stray, lose interest, close down? Why and in what ways does this loss of connectedness frequently happen with me?"

Or, instead of the *guilt* route, you may go for *accusation*, silently blaming the other for being so shallow, so boring, so demanding, so distracted, so unrelated, or so forth. Or you may blame the situation itself or the relationship for not offering enough. But we have already learned that guilt and accusation get in the way of unraveling complex here-and-now I-I interactions. *Here guilt and blame serve to disconnect us further from relating.* What kind of relatedness modes or patterns can be operating in the here-and-now of the relationship?

Considering the Thought Experiment and the Organizing experience

Involuntarily disconnecting this way happens to all of us in various ways all the time in relationships—but we seldom consciously focus on the process. At certain moments of building excitement, of increasing intimate connecting, we find ourselves feeling cautious, silently backpedaling, inexorably withdrawing, or allowing ourselves to wilt, to cringe, or to fall into disconnected reverie. We find ourselves withdrawing, jumping from thought to thought or blanking out entirely. And thereby—often much to our chagrin—inadvertently rupturing the developing links to whatever is occurring and to whatever might be able to happen.

Retreating from Contact and Intimacy:
Why Do We Resist Loving Contact?

If loving contact is what we desire most in relationships, how can we understand the universal resistance to intimate contact? Psychodynamically oriented psychotherapists now make the assumption that human minds are organized by relationships (*PDM* 2006, Norcross 2002). The mental and physical activities we engage in on a daily basis have been conditioned by the emotional relationships that have been available to us throughout a lifetime. When it comes to relationships, our more fortunate experiences have taught us to reach out hoping to find various kinds of loving connections. While our less fortunate experiences have taught us to fear and to retreat from certain kinds of intimate relationships. On the basis of our past experiences in relationships it stands to reason that we would naturally search out relationships which are likely to be good for us. And that we would avoid relationships which are likely to be bad for us.

Unfortunately, we do not choose our most significant relationships in this way! Why not? Because in our earliest months and years we all experienced disappointing, frustrating, and painful emotional relationships that influenced us in formative directions. As the twig is bent so grows the tree. As babies and growing children we learned a series of lessons about emotional relationships, which have been fundamental in organizing our personalities and in determining our choices in later relationships. We learn quickly how to mold ourselves to what we perceive to be important emotional realities around us. So that our most basic sense of safety and love soon resides in the familiar patterns of emotional exchange we learned from our first caregivers— no matter how self-limiting or self-abusive those patterns might appear to an objective observer (Lewis, et. al 2000). We are attracted to that which is familiar in relationships, not to that which might be good for us. We are vulnerable to repeating interpersonal emotional experiences that are known to us and are often oblivious to or neglectful of those possibilities that might be best for us but are unfamiliar (Hendrix 1988).

Therefore, when we find ourselves moving toward more intimacy in a relationship and then at some point we find ourselves silently backpedaling, the obvious inference is that some form of avoidance has been previously conditioned to this particular pathway to intimacy. The further inference is that at some similar previous juncture relationship-pain was encountered that was severe enough to post an unconscious signpost that says, "Never go there again!" What has been *transferred* from past experience is wariness or fear of certain kinds of intimate contact. What is being resisted is exposure to an intimate form of relationship that in our minds runs the risk of producing intense pain similar to relationship pain known in the past. What many people find surprising is that *our own minds actually produce intensely painful, aversive, and even confusing and disorienting experiences in order to warn us away from types of intimate contact and connection that have been known in the past to be disappointing or hurtful!* This warning usually operates automatically or unconsciously so that we are not aware of the signal pain or anxiety involved, but simply of a strong aversion to or a tendency to change the direction of the relating.

Summary

The term "Organizing" refers to the fundamental activity of Organizing a channel, a pathway, or a link to another human being that either,

(1) fails to take by virtue of unresponsiveness of the human relational environment thus giving rise to the first fear of no one being there, to the fear of being alone in the universe, or that

(2) aborts by virtue of the conditioned pain that prevents ongoing reciprocal connecting thus giving rise to the second fear of ever connecting again.

In either case the person is left perpetually Organizing a reaching channel toward others and then—based on transference and resistance learning—either

(1) withering out of discouragement or
(2) constricting out of fear.

Corollaries are that both varieties of "Organizing experience" are universal to a greater or lesser extent. And both kinds of Organizing transference form the universal foundations for all subsequent kinds of relational learning.

The Energy Arc Metaphor

A metaphor for further understanding the Organizing experience would be useful at this point. Imagine yourself in a lively interaction with another human being. Visualize an energy arc beginning where the other person's body touches the ground. The arc of energy rises to fill and animate the other person's body. The flow of the energy arc approaches you across the space between by way of the other person's eyes, voice, gestures, and emotional projections entering your body, animating it, and extending down to your own grounding. In a mutually enlivening engagement such as conversing, playing ball, dancing, or suckling the energy flows freely and reciprocally in both directions along the arc with each person being fully attuned to the life force within themselves while simultaneously responding to the lively emanations from the other person. An emotional union is achieved that is not reducible to stimulus-response analysis. It is through lively and enlivening participation and mutual engagement that human communication occurs and that consciousness of the cultural achievements of the human race are passed through the mind and body of an adult into the mind and body of a child. And later from one person to another.

But if this energy arc has not been experienced as sufficiently enlivening or has been experienced as the source of injury by an infant, she or he will fear being re-traumatized by again reaching out and being either disappointed or injured or both. The developing person who has been traumatically neglected or injured learns that human contact and connections are dangerous and to be avoided at all cost—turned away from, ruptured, broken, or abandoned by whatever means can be devised. By using the inventiveness and cleverness present in good cognitive and emotional intelligence, the person living

Organizing experiences soon learns a variety of ways of limiting interpersonal relationships so that they can be experienced as somewhat safe. The diversity and complexity of human intelligence allows people to avoid certain kinds of emotional relationships and to develop into fine human beings in many, if not most, ways. But intimate forms of relating deemed possibly dangerous and pain-producing are regularly avoided with accumulating consequences.

Notable among the unfortunate consequences are the tendencies to imitate human life (i.e. the mimical self) and to conform to human expectations (i.e. the false self) rather than to engage in the arduous task of negotiating the complexities of emotional-relatedness learning. As a result, the person may develop tendencies toward mania and/or depressive activities in order to join with or to avoid others—depending on the need, given her or his relational environment. Alternatively, the person may develop withdrawing, autistic, or schizoid tendencies in order to stay safely outside of the pale of dangerous human interactions. Or the person may develop what appear to others as unusual, persecutory, or bizarre thoughts and behaviors based on early cause and effect, approach-avoidance response patterns that originally had a motive to stay safely out of the way of interacting relationally with others perceived as frightening or dangerous. The person may have learned to dissociate one cognitive-emotional aspect of self from others in order to achieve a break in human connections, thus producing the sense of multiple personalities. Or compulsive and addictive patterns of consuming, holding, or evacuating various liquids, and solids or a habituation to other substances and behaviors may have evolved to serve the purposes of keeping the person out of contact with the human milieu or its representations. In short, trauma in the two earliest expressions of desire (for contact and/or connection) sets up relationship fears that serve to prevent, to rupture, or to limit sustained relating with other human beings. The cumulative effect over a lifetime is to limit or restrict a person's relationship intelligence. Substitute adaptive behavior patterns (called "symptoms" in psychiatry) are developed by the child which may permit her or him to "pass," to survive amidst a myriad of relational demands that are perceived as dangerous and to be avoided. Many people mask their relational disabilities by deliberately cultivating idiosyncratic or eccentric personalities. Otherwise, the person may develop apparently quite well until the person finds her- or himself in situations where relationship demands are unavoidable—such as school, dating, sex, work, or marriage and family.

Before leaving the energy arc metaphor for listening and responding to Organizing experiences I would like to point out that the arc can be broken in many places. The obvious place is between two people. And in research films of mothers and infants playing we often see the child actually looking away in moments of high stimulation— as if to process what she is experiencing. The patient mother waits for her attention to return. The insecure mother commences activities to get the child to look back at her. We note in therapy with Organizing transferences how often the client breaks contact within her own body with various somatic or psychological preoccupations. That is, imagine an infant standing to reach for mother's face—the legs can fail, something can distract, a fear can intervene, etc. Or, the client may have learned how to break the contact in the mind or body of the other, the therapist—"You know I sued my last therapist"—or some other equally distressing verbalization or activity.

Therapy with the Organizing experience

Psychotherapists study all of the relationships in a person's life for clues that will permit formulations about how the person regularly moves toward human contact and connection. And then how that person regularly accomplishes some—transference or resistance-based—form of interruption or breach, which prevents sustained mutual and reciprocal relatedness. "Where exactly in the arc of energetic enlivenment has the person learned to interrupt the relating and in how many different ways can the interruption be accomplished by this person?" are the questions of the therapist. When considered in this way the task of psychodynamic psychotherapy with Organizing experiences suddenly becomes clearer.

(1) The therapist must first spend considerable time and energy helping to establish an interpersonal atmosphere that the client can experience as somewhat safe.

(2) Next the therapist must encourage whatever forms of contact and connection the client can allow.

(3) Then the therapist must devise ways of holding the relating steady until the transferentially-determined resistance to relating appears.

(4) Finally, at the moment of interruption in the relationship a relational intervention is offered. The relational gesture is designed to communicate somehow: "I see that you believe that you must pull away from our emotional contact now…But that is not true. You have repeatedly established for yourself that I am a basically safe person to be with. So now, if you try, you can permit yourself to remain in connection with me a little longer than you might ordinarily allow with someone else…The compelling sensation that you are in grave danger,

that your body and mind may at any moment experience excruciating pain or fragmentation, that you are confused or lost, or that you must somehow compulsively pull away is essentially delusional no matter how real it feels...You have already established that I am safe to be with. You know that interactions with me can be useful and liberating. We have spoken of how terrifying it is for you to experience interpersonal intimacy in almost any form. You have the power to stay in connection with me now, despite your discomfort, restlessness, confusion, or terror...Contact between us can be safely tolerated for a little while longer. Try staying emotionally connected with me now so that we can see what further fears and demons lurk inside trying to pull you away, unnecessarily attempting to prevent your being hurt by our interaction...What do you feel in your body now? What shakiness, numbness, or terrors can you allow yourself to be aware of? Who am I to you at this moment? And how do you experience me and our relationship as a danger right now?

The working through of the Organizing transference consists of countless instances of encouraging the person in therapy to come to the brink of her or his sense of safety in the therapeutic relationship. And then for the therapist to find some concrete way of holding the person in emotional relationship a moment longer—long enough for some unsettling or terrifying reaction to emerge so it can be known and processed within the relationship.

The key feature here is for the therapist to encourage connection while simultaneously recognizing the terror being created by the attempt. I have written about the potential usefulness of token physical contact—such as touching fingers, holding hands, locking eye contact, demanding full voice contact or other concrete forms of contact—for the purpose of holding the connection so that the transferential terror can become known. In Appendix A I provide my "informed consent for limited physical contact" as an explanation for and a model of how a therapist might choose to work through such delicate moments with a client. Discussing with the client in advance what moments of interpersonal contact might look like and having a well-understood informed consent in place create safety nets for the otherwise risky process of elucidating primitive transference experiences through relational interventions.

Optimal Responsiveness with the Organizing experience

Optimal responsiveness required to work successfully in the area of Organizing experience begins with the establishment of a safe interpersonal environment, which can take from months to years to accomplish. The therapist gently but persistently encourages movement toward dynamic emotional relatedness. The therapist remains constantly alert for subtle (and many times not so subtle) signs of an emotional retreat that signal the arrival of disengaging transference and a possible moment for a relational intervention. Optimal responsiveness to the Organizing experience entails a realization on the part of the therapist that interpersonal emotional contact and connection transferentially warns the client of an imminent re-traumatization, so that the person quickly moves into some safety-searching, contact-avoidant activity (or symptom). If the therapist is prepared and moves quickly enough she or he may be able to seize the moment of retreat with a verbal or nonverbal relational intervention that prevents the rupture of the emotional contact now being experienced. And of the terror, numbness, or retreat mechanism which is serving to avoid or rupture emotional contact. From a technique standpoint the client can be forewarned of the importance of such moments. And forewarned that the therapist will attempt some relational intervention at such moments in order to hold the interpersonal contact steady whenever the therapist senses it slipping. The forewarned client may then be willing to sustain the relating momentarily in order to experience whatever forms of pain, withdrawal, numbness, fragmentation, confusion, or terror may ensue so that two can experience them together.

Working Through the Organizing Transference and Resistance

The working through process consists of therapist and client learning together over time how to *catch in the moment the transferentially-based resistance to sustained emotional contact and connection*. And learning how to hold these contactful moments together through whatever body-mind-relationship-relationship reactions of terror, numbness, fragmentation, and/or confusion may occur in one or the other or both body-mind-relationships. Studying together characteristic modes of resistance to contact enacted by both participants allows both to be watching for the special ways connection is being avoided. It may be helpful to study the approach-avoidance patterns participated in by two in terms of basic fight, flight, and freeze reactions. It will also likely be interesting to notice how the client not only breaks contact within her or his body and between two bodies, but also how the client arranges to break the reciprocal energy arc in the mind and body of the therapist by precipitating various countertransference reactions. Accusatory "clamoring for more," "demanding better attunement," or "insisting upon needed kinds of responsiveness" often become ways of disrupting the therapist in such a way that the interaction or "interacting energy arc" is broken in the body-mind-relationship of the therapist! (Hedges, 1994a, c, 2000).

Varieties of Common Countertransference Relational Experience

I. Organizing Level: confusion, fragmentation, withdrawal, and/or distractibility when connections are avoided or ruptured

II. Symbiotic Level: unusual, untoward, perverse, rageful, and/or unbounded responses to projected scenarios and role-reversal scenarios

III. Selfother Level: facilitating boredom, drowsiness, and/or irritation at having one's own narcissistic needs neglected or thwarted

IV. Triangular Relatedness: overstimulating or intrusive sexual and aggressive reactions that threaten to interfere with or act as an impediment to the ongoing development of the client's material

Four Kinds of Countertransference to the Organizing experience

Different forms of countertransference experience—that is, emotional responsiveness on the part of the analyst—are to be expected, depending upon the developmental level of the issues currently being presented for analysis. (See Hedges (1992) for a study of the variety of kinds of countertransference responsiveness.) Four distinct forms of countertransference have emerged with clarity that characterize therapists' responsiveness to Organizing experience:

1. Denial of human potential. The most common form of countertransference has seen Organizing personalities as witches, evildoers, hopelessly psychotic, and in other ways not quite human. In this attitude is a denial of human potential and a denial of the possibility of being able to stimulate desire in such a way as to reawaken it and to

analyze blocks to human relating. We hear: "I can't reach you—you are too sick. You are untreatable, so we will lock you up or give you drugs to sedate or pacify you."

2. Fear of primitive energy. When an analytic therapist invites the Organizing experience into a transference relationship, he or she is asking that the full impact of primitive aggressive and sexual energies of the client be directed squarely at the person of the therapist. Therapists fear the power of this experience because it can be quite disorienting and, if not carefully assessed and monitored, potentially dangerous. But fear of basic human affectivity is irrational, and we now have at our disposal many rational ways of inviting and managing the Organizing level affects and energies.

3. Encountering our own Organizing experiences. When we as therapists invest ourselves emotionally in reaching out again and again to a client only to be repeatedly abandoned or refused, it stimulates our own most primitive experiences of reaching out to our own mothers during our Organizing developmental period, hoping for a response and feeling traumatized when the desired response was not forthcoming. Our own "psychotic mother" transference can reappear projected onto the client as we attempt to provide systematic and sustained connection for people living Organizing states. How each of us as individual practitioners develops staying power is the crucial question.

4. Empathy leading to breaks in contact. After the preliminary phases are well under way, we notice the client begins excitedly to see in outside contacts (as well as in the therapy hour) how the breaking of contact is being

regularly accomplished. They begin a valiant struggle to maintain contact nearly everywhere they go—especially with the therapist. The therapist sense that the relating is "too much too soon" and titrates the emotional intimacy empathically.

Case Studies of the Organizing experience

What follows are two long-term case studies conducted by myself and Dr. Audrey Seaton-Bacon that illustrate the working through of the Organizing Transference. Further reading would include my three books on the topic. *In Search of the Lost Mother of Infancy* features eight long-term case studies contributed by eight different Southern California therapists with my teaching of theory and technique interspersed. The full theory of the Organizing Transference is laid down in *Working the Organizing experience: Transforming Psychotic, Schizoid, and Autistic States,* into which numerous case examples and commentary are inserted. And *Terrifying Transferences: Aftershocks of Childhood Trauma*, which provides twelve examples of long-term working through of the Organizing transference, contributed by twelve different therapists with commentary by myself.

Case Study: Lawrence Hedges: Paul's Organizing Transference

A year into therapy and following a lively discussion about Paul's parents and some difficult relationships he was having at work Paul and I began to formulate some important aspects of his Organizing transference.

Paul: As people encounter me, I subtly behave in ways so as to discourage or at least not to encourage the connection. I feel this scary, paranoid distortion and I am unable to bridge it by showing kindness, warmth, or generosity or by being at ease with the other person. In this distortion I feel that they don't like me, or that they want to use me, to abuse me, or to cheat me. I then subtly withdraw. This so clearly comes from my relationship with Louise.

Larry: I hear you saying that when a person, perhaps even a neutral person, who neither loves nor hates you moves into your life and is giving neutral or perhaps even lukewarm "getting acquainted" responses, your paranoid delusions take over and you feel that they hate you or want you dead—like with Louise.

Paul: And then I am stuck. I can't go across any bridges. My distortion makes me afraid, and so we play a standoff game. I'm scared of them and they of me. Unless that person clearly and affirmatively reaches out we are not sure if we can trust each other. I can't initiate warmth and generosity, no way. The best people can see of me is that I'm withdrawn and scared—even if they see I have an honest intent.

Larry: It's not just that you're shy and afraid?

Paul: No. I'm clearly forbidden to reach out. It's as though there is a force field from outer space that paralyzes my brain. Injecting terrified anxiety feelings into me. An outside force setting up an overriding terror which totally prevents me from sharing intimately, warmly, generously, affectionately, or presenting myself in a positive light. I have to be passive, awaiting their judgments and pronouncements on me, which are bound to be bad. Even if their estimations of me aren't negative at first, I make them bad. I actively make people see me in a bad light. That's the important part—I force people to see me as bad.

Larry: I have the image of two people with neutral or lukewarm feelings toward one another, wanting to get to know each other, and slowly approaching each other as though they are getting ready to do a relationship dance. It's as if there are invisible tendrils of relatedness silently reaching out...

Paul: (Interrupting) And I have scissors that snip them off!

Larry: But how is this accomplished?

Paul: I interrupt. I don't let people finish their sentences. I give people the cold shoulder. I make them see me as a miserable wreck. I make them hate me.

Larry: You are telling me that you actually cut off what might become a warm flow between you and someone else of ideas and feelings. You cut off the tendrils of relationship, because of the Leonard and Louise living inside. You snip off the connections. The Louise you identified with in infancy, who is still living inside of you, has snipped those connections, has forced the relatedness flow to stop. You are saying that you comply with the inner Louise's instructions to destroy the interpersonal links, the potential tendrils of real connection which might allow for friendship and love. Alternatively, you make people somehow feel cut off from you, confused, or lost track of.[2]

The Banquet of Flesh: A Central Relational Image

Paul has many ways of devaluing himself in personal interactions with his recurring belief that others see him as an ineffective, weak, confused, miserable wreck. The images, the people involved, and the negative qualities vary considerably, but the downward spiral of Paul's line of self-criticism during many sessions invariably drones on in a similar vein ending with the surprise line directed at me—"and you think so too!" The accusation effectively ruptured any sense of connection we had at the time because I felt regularly obligated to address it.

By the time we had spent three years together I had gone through various phases of responding to this challenge regularly thrown at me. In the early phases I would protest that I had no such view, that in fact I liked him very much, saw him as quite competent, and respected him in every way, and so forth—depending on whatever barrage of self-criticism he had just unleashed and whatever I could honestly state at the moment. But Paul always "had" me in some way or another because he could quickly quote something potentially critical that I had indeed said earlier in the session or on some previous occasion. He would give the line a deadly negative twist to prove that I indeed did think ill of him. That he was right, that it was true that I saw him as a sloppy miserable wretch or/as a ne'er do well too.

At first I would go into momentary confusion at Paul's seemingly deliberate misinterpretation of what I had said. Then I learned to confront him and to dispute what he was imputing to me—and then to reaffirm him. But these downward spirals of self-criticism followed by a gauntlet thrown to me continued. At times I tried to go with whatever negativity might have been implicit in my former comments. But then I would attempt to show Paul that my meaning was essentially positive—but he would remain unconvinced, nonplussed, or skeptical. After a while I got frustrated and tried to point out the double bind Paul put me in on these occasions. At other times I would get angry with Paul insisting that he was deliberately distorting what I had said or done—just to irritate me! Then I would try to show what his motivation might be for needing to see me as a harsh critic of his at this particular point in time. I tried various ways of exploring meanings, of looking for contextual cues and of attempting to align Paul on the side of studying the interaction—all to little avail. Something critical was not yet understood. Whenever I was indeed impatient or irritated I did my best to cop to it, but mere acknowledgement of my ill feelings toward Paul struck him as superficial and forced. I saw him as a needy wretched creature, hated him, and wanted him dead—that was that.

Eventually I could feel myself squarely in Paul's trap every time he laid it. I simply lapsed into looking at him inquisitively in response, trying to get him to elaborate what had just transpired between us and why. Paul wasn't uncooperative in these searches for meaning, but he always somehow got back to the refrain that I indeed hated him and I that I had said it clearly in so many words, no matter how much I tried to deny it. Of course we tried in vain various transpositions of Louise and Leonard transference, all of which led up to the following events.

After a particularly social but frustrating weekend Paul had the following dream:

> I was going somewhere with Jerry (whose passivity all weekend had messed up a series of plans). Like we were in some European city, maybe Paris, and were supposed to be going to eat at this rather elegant cafe or restaurant. When we arrived we were shown the sideboard where two live horses were laid out, sedated with their eyes covered so they couldn't see what was happening. We were handed these knives or meat cleavers and a plate in a nonchalant way. Like what you were supposed to do for your dining pleasure in this elegant bistro was to chop off chunks of meat—live

flesh to eat. Like it was supposed to be some sort of delicacy and we were expected to simply go along with it. I recognized the scene as bizarre, as something I simply didn't want to do. I was immediately nervous and began looking around, like maybe there was some vegetarian dish instead! I woke up very upset and began thinking about my relationship with Leonard.

In Paul's associations to the dream he emphasized the element of passivity, that he was simply expected to go along with this horse's ass kind of banquet. He and Leonard are always taking chunks out of each other's flesh and it's supposed to be okay, the proper and pleasurable way to relate. In the dream the two horses are laid out, sedated, and blindfolded so they won't actually see or feel what is being done to them (the passive position). Paul could see that the underpinning was, of course, the scenarios with Louise in which each had to be the destruction of the other—but both pretended that everything was as it should be. Paul said that he has always felt forced to passively comply with this bizarre and monstrous feasting on flesh that was in vogue in his family.

My interpretations focused in a congratulatory way on Paul's actively deciding to turn away from his life-long pattern of feasting on flesh—this scenario of mutual cannibalism—to something different, namely to nourishing and healthy vegetables. We processed this dream in a variety of ways for several sessions.

A week later Paul started into another one of his downward spirals of self-criticism. By now well-accustomed to the horror of watching Paul rip himself limb from limb in these tirades, I watched with the fresh image of a flesh-eating banquet in the back of my mind. This time I saw the gauntlet coming a good three minutes before it landed squarely in front of me. I was lying in wait, in almost open-mouthed amazement, watching Paul's downward spiral of self-effacement with horror, knowing he would soon launch his surprise attack on me. I wish I could remember the exact content, but I was swimming in the increasing intensity of the moment. Paul suddenly looked up directly at me and said his usual, "and you think so too." But I was ready. I went with it this time. I continued his vicious, destructive banter along the same content he had just provided me with. I told him with full intention and affect that it was true that I hated him, that he was indeed worthless, psychotic, delusional, despicable, a miserable wretch, and so forth. Paul was stunned. But grasping my ploy, he quickly added, "you take your pleasure and amusement from watching me tear myself down and slowly self-destruct."

I immediately fell into a dark pit. In this quick and brief exchange we had deepened the emotional material to a horrifyingly new low. At some level I knew instantly that his accusation was true, whether I was consciously aware of it or not. Then Paul added, "and you do it so you can feel secure in your superiority." I was truly stunned. I remember thinking, "I have to go here. This is about me. I have to let myself feel all of this." And I did. As the two of us sat in momentary silence I let my body and my mind drop into the experience of taking my pleasure and amusement from watching Paul self-efface and self-destruct in front of my very eyes. I had to actively let myself enjoy his misery and pain so that I could feel secure in my superiority. Sinking rapidly, I got there—and I enjoyed it. I actually allowed a full sense of cannibalistic glee and destructiveness to overcome me. Paul tried to talk—but I waved him off to shut him up. My mind swam in timeless delight and horror—images of Caesars languishing in decadent delight in the

Roman Circus swirled. I saw slaves being slaughtered and eaten alive by lions. I thought of Nero, of Rome Burning, of Hitler, of lines of Jews, the ovens, of Sade, of naked savages chewing on human bones, of children being mercilessly beaten, of psychotics being tortured by mindless gambits of sadistic therapists. Tears welled up in my eyes. My stomach churned in violent upheaval. I stammered trying to speak what I was experiencing—voice quaking, facing the wide-eyed Paul.

I slowly came to myself; "I can't do it! I won't do it! I refuse this God-forsaken banquet of flesh—show me the vegetables!" We laughed but were both taken aback—shaken by the truth and violence of the moment and by our mutual willingness to go there. Vegetables were a welcome comic relief.

"As a child, Paul, you had no choice. You were led to this flesh-eating banquet by the parents that you loved and trusted and then you were expected to partake. It was all that was offered. You had no way of knowing that there was a better way. You were drugged and blinded and told to eat. But I'm not a child. Nor am I passive. This flesh-eating banquet you lead me to is a bizarre horror and I will have nothing to do with it. I will not eat!"

I had to repeat the lines forcefully several times to rescue myself from the dizziness and emotional pull of the sadomasochistic pit, the swirling horrors, the timeless spinning, and the disgusting nausea of destruction. "I saw it. I felt it. It was terrifyingly real and horrible. I won't go there with you. I absolutely will not!" But, of course, I had in fact already gone there with him.

When Paul was wakened from the dream by his refusal to be passively led into cannibalizing on chunks of flesh, I understood his anxiety as his fear of turning away from the table that has always been laid for him. When Paul tried once again to take me to that bizarre flesh-eating banquet table, I finally grasped at an experiential body level what has been perhaps Paul's deepest truth. Terrified, horrified, I yelled, "horse's ass, I won't go there with you!" Paul and I were together at last. We both were refusing in our relationship to be passively traumatized by our internalized sadomasochistic parents.

Paul has for a lifetime feared relationships based on the template of a drugged and blinded cannibalistic scenario. He has experienced his emotional relationship with me according to the same pattern of abusive horrors. But until now Paul has been compelled to return repeatedly to being the self-destructing sacrifice for his internal parents' amusement, pleasure, and self-aggrandizement. It was the only way of emotionally relating that Paul had ever learned, the only way of connecting to me that he knew. To connect meant to experience humiliating, self-abusive, masochistic surrender. For a lifetime intimate emotional relationships had been systematically avoided. To disconnect from all human contact is paramount to withering and dying. I had to experience with Paul the horror of my own deep psychological images and the ways in which I too sadistically cannibalized him—made my livelihood, took my self-satisfaction and security, off of his mutilated living flesh and blood. We were both sobered by the experience we had created together; the experience that told a truth we had neither before dared to articulate. Paul's deep pattern was yielding at last—and mine as well.

Case Study: Audrey Seaton-Bacon: "I Am Going to Die"

You are about to encounter two years of very difficult work begun at a doctoral-level training clinic by Audrey Seaton-Bacon who carried her work with Anne Marie into private practice after graduation.

65

"Will you sit by me?" "Will you hold my hand?" "Can I lean on you?" "Will you hold me?" "Please don't hurt me!" "Help me!" "I can't find you!" "I'm scared!" "What's happening to me?" "I can't make it!" "I have to hit myself." *"I am going to die."*

These statements and questions expressed the need and the terror that Anne Marie felt as she and Audrey immersed themselves into the depths of her internalized Organizing experience.

Training to be a therapist rarely prepares students for this type of intense need, this regressed and frightening demand for closeness that is destined to stir up feelings of destruction and self-destruction. In fact, training supervisors are often so preoccupied with teaching "correct technique" and malpractice concerns that clients with such primitive needs are often overlooked or severely neglected. Says Audrey Seaton-Bacon:

> For Anne Marie, the terror came in her reaching out for connection. She had not been emotionally connected with anyone for much, if not most, of her life. She struggled to be emotionally present. Physical contact was the only way she knew how to, and could, stay present. She regressed back into what seemed to be her first month of life. With wide-eyed innocence and intensity, she searched for the other—me. Her reaching out produced fears of being hurt, abandoned, dropped, and dying. Her body betrayed her with memories she could not identify and memories of being sexually abused. She recoiled. She reached. She recoiled and reached until, several months into the process, we made contact. The connection we finally achieved was immensely satisfying to both of us. It was intense with aliveness. All our senses betrayed us. We giggled. We watched each other. We

imitated each other. We played. We found each other. We
disconnected. (pp. 186-7)

When Audrey was asked to write up this case for publication she
reports that she found herself spoiling—minimizing, destroying, and
ignoring—the request. She feared exposing her own struggles that
were going on in the depth of the transference/countertransference
entanglement.

Anne Marie had attempted therapy several times before to address
her history of childhood sexual abuse, anorexia, and bulimia. After an
abortive attempt at marital counseling she was ready for deep
individual therapy. In the early months of therapy Anne Marie talked
of "feeling shaky inside," her fear of being hurt, and her feelings of
being empty.

Anne Marie related intellectually, but not affectively, with others
in her life. When she did finally begin to experience emotions, they
were ambitendent—i.e., alternating good and bad feelings of equal
intensity. She reported feeling that she does not belong anywhere, but
as the work took shape she began to experience the intensity of her
own neediness and quickly grew more dependent on Audrey. Her
critical attitude toward her neediness and dependency was interpreted
as her internalized parents' response to her neediness, and as an overall
attempt to prevent or break any connection she made with Audrey.

As Anne Marie regressed, she demanded more of me.
There were times that she struggled to find me. Sitting across
from her seemed too far out of reach. She asked me to sit
beside her. She needed me closer, but the closeness triggered
memories from her past. She struggled to stay present. She
reached her hand out for me to hold in a desperate attempt to

stay present. I held on feeling helpless and conflicted. She flinched. The body memories were present. She cried. She wanted me to make it stop. I couldn't. I reminded her that they were memories of an earlier attempt to reach out. She kept reaching until the body memories subsided. …Any outside noise or voice startled her, and some frightened her away. At this point in the process, Anne Marie needed more frequent contact. Weekly sessions were increased from one to three, and daily five-minute phone contacts were added. (p. 188)

Changes terrified Anne Marie as the transference of unpredictable, abandoning Mom and abusive Dad became a part of the therapeutic relationship. After Anne Marie had tested and determined that Audrey cared for her and was there to stay, she became very playful in the sessions and brought in children's storybooks for her therapist to read to her.

Anne Marie is the oldest of four girls. At the age of 5 months, she moved with her parents to another state. The move, Anne Marie was later told, was very traumatic for her as she cried and screamed in terror during the three-day journey. She had been told that she had intractable vertigo and was inconsolable. One year later, her sister was born setting off rivalry immediately. Her sister could be held and seemed to receive all the parental love that Anne Marie desperately wanted but pushed away. With the birth of two more sisters Anne Marie's wish for parental acceptance, love, recognition, and presence became more faint. Verbal messages were contradictory: "I am here for you, but I can't be" and "You can count on me, but I am too busy." Although she was uncertain as to its onset and frequency, Anne Marie reported being sexually abused by her father until the age of 13.

At 26 she married, believing this to be her salvation from a life of inner isolation. But immediately after the wedding, Anne Marie reported experiencing a recapitulation of the emotional abandonment and abuse of her parent-child relationship. Once again she was alone. She had no real friendships. She stated, "Everyone I let myself get close to, reach out to, leaves...hurts me."

Anne Marie quickly replicated the duality of her parental relationship with Audrey. She voiced her need for relationship, but then consistently emotionally distanced herself. At any point of connection she reported shaky feelings as she struggled to control her emerging emotions. She cried, "I don't belong anywhere." And she reported feeling very young, "like an infant." For a while she stopped talking. She had no words. She was angry that Audrey sat across from her like an authority figure who could control her. She became extremely critical and verbally harsh with herself. She coiled her adult body into a small ball—a fetal position—and cried. Anne Marie's silent sobs came from deep within her, a place unfamiliar to both of them at the time. Between sessions, she phoned feeling "panicked, trapped, and in terror." Her anxiety grew as she came to the office.

> She was afraid of the unknown and so was I, but for different reasons. She did not know what to do with the infusion of emotions she was having or how to make sense of her regressed state, and I was intensely afraid of the parental transference that was being established. At this point in the process, I became cognizant that we were working with psychotic or Organizing elements in the transference that were unpredictable. Was I safe? Was she safe? Words fail to fully describe the terror experienced by

both parties in the primitive transference-countertransference relationship. (p. 192)

Anne Marie's initial anxiety in coming to Audrey's office was intense. Attempts to contain her anxiety through deep breathing and making herself comfortable on the couch resulted in an influx of strong emotions and a cascading regression. Anne Marie grew aware of these unidentified, fused emotions, and attempted to get away from them—to detach. She described feelings of numbness in her hands and an intense need to get away. This, she said, was the way she felt when her father had come into her room at night. Now she wanted to flee from Audrey as the father she could not get away from. She had many body memories. She felt physical pain. "Audrey, what's happening to me?" She became totally numb physically and reported being mentally lost. Audrey reports feeling helpless to ease the pain even as she worked hard to reassure Anna Marie that she was not in fact being abused, that she was Audrey and not Father. But headlines raced through her head. "Client Accuses Therapist of Sexual Abuse." How easily blurred the boundary between the memories of the past and the present transference reality can become. Audrey understood it was important for Anne Marie to contact the abusive father who lived within, and through the transference to experience her therapist as him abusing her. "It felt awful to watch and experience Anne Marie's pain, and to feel like the perpetrator. I was relieved at the end of the session. I was emotionally drained." Anne Marie was also emotionally drained. Unable to move or drive, she lay in the next office for about two hours before leaving.

The above episode opened the door to a whole new way of doing therapy. Anne Marie grew relentless in her challenges and demands as she felt certain that she was on the right track. In the next session she reported feeling "broken, alone, isolated, and physically cold." She asked Audrey to sit beside her on the couch and to hold her. Audrey responds, "It's much more comfortable in my chair across from you. What you need and what is comfortable for me in my professional posture are not the same." Later Audrey realizes that Anne Marie was asking for her to be physically near, to be real, to be present. "While I understood the need therapeutically, it felt as if she had asked me to step out on a plank that dangled over a bottomless pool of gurgling lava. I sat next to her and she appeared to have moments of what I thought at the time seemed to be dissociation. I later came to understand these times as moments of interpersonal disconnection which were brought about by her longing for and/or achieving intimate contact."

Audrey's physical presence during her disconnections helped to ground Anne Marie to the present, but triggered Audrey's own childhood asthmatic condition. She struggled to breathe. She wanted to get away. Anne Marie was too close. *The more she reached out for me, the more difficult it was for her and for me to stay emotionally present.* We were both terrified of connecting."

Anne Marie also seemed to treasure any personal information she learned about her therapist. Initially, Audrey was concerned and felt uncomfortable about disclosing personal information. This was not her usual mode of operating.

> However, as she and I moved toward connection, I realized that, as with any healthy relationship, her questions developed out of genuine interest and a need to know rather than entitlement. One question was about my birthday. She remembered the month as a result of leftover items from a staff celebration last year, but did not know the day. Initially,

when she asked, I declined to tell her. She accepted my choice but could not hide the hurt. She gave me a birthday card and a little flowerpot (quite symbolic in our work) for my desk. She wanted to celebrate my birthday as it was important to her—I was important to her. Eventually, I shared my birth date and took in her care for me. I took her in and became more vulnerable to her. She, in turn, was able to take me in and connect with me at a much deeper level of relatedness. (p. 195)

As the two moved toward more relatedness, Anne Marie continued to regress. She emotionally and verbally reached out for Audrey, then pushed her away. Audrey interpreted her terror in making the connection. Sometimes she sat curled up on the couch with her head buried in a blanket that she wrapped protectively around herself. At other times she placed the pillows around herself to form a barricade. As memories of her father plagued her, incidents of bingeing and purging became a therapeutic issue. Her regressions initially took the form of an angry teen, a helpless child, and then a terrified infant. Audrey sat next to her to help her stay present.

Her request for physical contact, for hugs at the end of the sessions and/or to be held, was another crisis point in our work. Throughout my training, I have taken a conservative position about touch. My position grew out of my desire to stay far away from anything that could be misconstrued by a client. However, the more I learned about individuals working in the Organizing level of development, the more I learned about the potential therapeutic value of touch. My hesitation and cautions, although well-founded and appropriate, slowed her regression work. Anne Marie responded to my hesitation with anger. She felt rejected. She and I had many talks about the therapeutic purpose of touch, which was solely to help her stay present. She read, signed, and discussed an informed consent contract regarding the use of touch in the therapeutic process (see Hedges 1994c, and Appendices D and E of this book). Overall, she felt that touch helped her to stay present, to know that she was not alone, and that someone cared.

Holding her hand, allowing her to rest her head on a pillow in my lap, allowing her to lean on me, holding her and/or giving her a hug during or at the end of our sessions, would convey my presence more than my words. On one occasion, I denied her a hug as it seemed that her desire was less to stay in contact and more to soothe bad feelings that arose in the session. I wanted her to know that I was still there, and that she did not have to get rid of her bad feelings. (pp 195-6)

Over time, Anne Marie became more aware that her longings and needs were not bad, but that the perceived or actual injuries that she experienced in her initial reaching out to satisfy her needs caused her to recoil and emotionally split off, and to detach her emotional self. As she reached, body memories became more painful. She would scream, most often without sound and sometimes with screeching cries, whimpering, and intense sobbing. She would twist and turn her body, pushing an unseen something from her face, wiping her face, kicking or recoiling into a ball, barricading herself with the pillows on the couch, pulling the blanket tight around her—covering every inch, and then end suddenly in a frozen state. She was unable to move, breathe, or swallow. When her eyes would open, they were empty. She was gone.

Once Audrey realized that these body memories were representations of her past traumas and *serving the internalized psychotic mother who kept her from connections*, Audrey would talk more to her during these times and/or hold her hand so that she could feel her presence.

> The internalized psychotic mother is described by Hedges (1994c) as the internalized representation of the traumatizing other experienced during early attempts to connect. I talked, in part because I felt helpless and wanted her to know that I was there, and also because Anne Marie, when she was able, asked me to keep talking. Talking and holding her hands or her, she reported later, helped her to maintain her awareness of me and facilitated brief moments of connection. (p. 197)

Finally, in one session, the terror in the connection stopped for a few minutes. Anne Marie had asked for and had been granted permission to lean on Audrey's shoulder. She exhaled and settled. She had allowed herself to be emotionally held. Both knew it. She felt small—an infant. It was peaceful. It felt wonderful. She left the office that day with a borrowed teddy bear as she attempted to hold on to that place in which she found the (m)other.

The transference relationship with mother included feelings of betrayal, distance, unpredictability, and "never being there" or "being there but not there." In addressing these issues inherent in the transference, Audrey observed her resistance to taking in the good and in allowing herself to be emotionally comforted by it. She began to use infant analogies more frequently. Audrey described her as a colicky baby who was fussing and kicking so much that she was unaware of mother's presence, or that she was being held. Given this picture of herself, she would attempt to settle herself.

As she settled herself and moved once again toward connection, and then again Anne Marie began to experience what she termed as "strange feelings." Somatic memories intensified. She reported being scared and feeling frozen. The predefensive reactions flight or freeze, were present in her relationship with her parents and were being recapitulated in the therapeutic relationship. Her emotions were very frightening to her. She feared being dependent. After an extraordinary internal battle with the vulnerable, infant self, she allowed herself to regress once more.

She sat on the couch and her adult body behaved in ways characteristic of an infant. She sat with her face turned into the couch, or against Audrey's arm, with movements that resembled rooting. During this phase, her use of the teddy bear was critical in maintaining the connection. Periodically she asked Audrey to spray the teddy bear with her perfume. She had connected though touch, hearing, and now smelling—infant senses.

However this place of safe and trusting connection ended when Audrey informed Anne Marie that she would be unavailable during an upcoming weekend. There was rage, head banging, hitting herself and abusing the teddy bear. She felt she had done something wrong or was bad. She was enraged that she had allowed herself to embrace Audrey and felt responsible for her leaving. In a very small voice from somewhere deep inside her, she pleaded, "Don't leave me." She reluctantly accepted reassurances that it would only be a weekend and that Audrey would be back on Monday.

In subsequent sessions Anne Marie did everything she could to create a breach and Audrey found herself feeling lightheaded, dizzy, and sleepy. In the countertransference she felt guilty for causing such pain.

Anne Marie continued to become more present and began to sustain connection for longer periods of time. The two moved from experiencing only moments of connection to her being able to stay connected and hold on to Audrey for a day at a time. She talked about the good feelings she had in finding and being able to sustain connection. At one point she described her feeling as "joy." It seemed that the more present she became the more difficult it was for her to tolerate any breaks in the process.

When Audrey announced her vacation Anne Marie became frozen with fear. She said that she felt as if she were left out for a truck to run over. In her terror, she asked Audrey not to leave. The body memories, the physical coldness, the all-bad self, and the suicidal ideation all returned in full force. This was a very difficult time for Audrey as she fought being identified with the all-bad mother who abandoned her child when she was needed.

> The professional and personal support system I had established helped me to navigate my way through this arduous place. Anne Marie withdrew emotionally and challenged me verbally about everything. Initially, she minimized the items given to her as aids to maintain connection with me, as well as a phone call I made and a postcard I sent while I was on vacation. Later, she talked of the importance of the items in my absence, but spoiled her care and need for me through creating a good-bad split

between me and the good-bad therapist she worked with during my absence. (p. 206)

Then came the ultimate attempt to stop the process and destroy any connection that was there. Anne Marie violated her verbal agreement not to leave her young daughter at her parents' home. They had agreed that as a state mandated reporter, Audrey would have to report any behavior that would place a child at risk for abuse, particularly with a known offender. Consequently, they had agreed that Anne Marie would not leave her daughter at her parents' home for babysitting or any other purpose.

At first, it seemed that Anne Marie's violation of the agreement was a careless act. But it soon became apparent that she was quite aware of the risk involved. Anne Marie lamented, "This is not like me." It soon became clear that this was an all-out attempt to destroy the connection Audrey had with her infant self. Anne Marie—the infant self—was connecting with Audrey, and the internalized psychotic parent was summoned to stop it at any cost as the memories and trauma associated with father were being relived in the transference.

Audrey somewhat reluctantly filed the required abuse report and she and Anne Marie continued to process the terror she felt in connecting that very vulnerable, needy part of herself with Audrey. This seemed to have been a turning point to a deeper level of processing. Thereafter Anne Marie's dreaming became more regular and reflected her internal life—her searching, her struggle, her needs, her fears, and her truth. The following is an excerpt from one of her dreams:

I want to bathe but don't want to take off my clothes or towel—they are staring and I can tell they mean me harm—appear nice but the comments and body language tell me to stay away.... Then a door opens and a pregnant woman comes out, the women are mean and threaten her—tell her to go back and do what they tell her if she doesn't want to get hurt—she goes back and continues to wipe the shower down with paper towels—comes back to them—it's not good enough, then they want something else done—nothing is ever going to please them—I can feel they aren't going to let her go—suddenly she balks—doesn't do what they want and they grab her and take a long broom-like stick and shove it inside her—I'm terrified—I know she'll lose her baby.

Then I am in another place with others around and there is a woman having a baby—but it's too young—it's too small—I know it is—I hear someone say "We can try to save it"—but I know it's too little—could hold it in one hand—the mother—something is happening with her—her mouth—surgery? repairing it? The baby is held up and then gone...
(p. 208)

Anne Marie's dream, an internalization of her childhood realities, reflected the lack of safety in her internal world. It identified a world marked by threats, penetration, attempted abortion, and a life-and-death struggle to survive. She feared that the self that she is giving birth to, that vulnerable part of herself, was too small—too young to survive. *She had always lived in constant and terrifying dread that she was going to die. At last her deepest fear of being connected was represented in the dream as well as the transference, that if she stays connected her nascent self is going to abort and die.*

"Anne Marie taught me that she is the master of her ship, the creator of her future, and I, much like a parent, simply provide and maintain a healthy and safe environment for her to grow in—to metamorphose into the fully functioning being that she was meant to be" (p. 209.)

Summary of the Organizing experience

The "Organizing experience" refers to the earliest human desire to organize channels for contact and connection—first with the maternal body and later with the maternal mind. And to the corresponding re-living of primitive terrors of being painfully and life-threateningly alone in the universe and/or of being injured as a result of interpersonal connections. The specific fears associated with reaching for contact and connection are transferred into later relationships and serve as resistance to certain or all kinds of interpersonal intimacy. Through projective identification as well as dissociation and mutual enactments both client and therapist become immersed in not yet formulated experiences. The goal of relational interventions in psychotherapy with the Organizing experience is to demonstrate in word, deed, and action that the transferred terror of contact and connection is essentially delusional—as it is based on early developmental experiences and not on the current possibilities for rewarding intimate relating. I would, however, add that in the process of working through, each participant is living in part with unformulated, dissociated experiences and multiple self-states that become mutually enacted in the transference-countertransference matrix. The work of the Interpersonal/relational psychoanalyst Donnel

Stern studies the therapeutic processes being spoken of here from somewhat different but compatible angles (Stern 1997, 2010, in press).

Part III

Borderline Personality Organization

Introduction: Enactments in Replicated Symbiotic Scenarios

Psychotherapists have had a keen interest in developmental theories since Abraham (1924) defined the psychosexual stages, Erikson (1959) set up the stages of ego development, and Mahler put forth her separation-individuation theory of development (1968). The assumption of these early attempts at developmental listening was that symptoms and transferences in adult psychotherapy could be traced back to the individual's developmental experiences in infancy and childhood.

Edith Jacobson (1954, 1964) shifted the paradigm from considering individual growth experiences *per se* to looking at the ways children in their early years come to internally represent their worlds of self and other and how those internal representations of relationships serve as silent guides in subsequent relational experiences. She was explicitly aware that the word "representation" was metapsychological and that what she was reaching for was *the child's ongoing experiences as limited or constricted by past relational experiences*. Following in her footsteps, Kernberg (1976, 1980) saw the building blocks of personality as (1) a representation of self, (2) a representation of other, and (3) an affect state relationally linking them—again, a crucial step toward recognizing what would later be called the interpersonal or intersubjective field and how freedom in the field is systematically limited by prior constricting experiences.

Hedges' (1983) four relatedness Listening Perspectives are derived from Mahler's and Jacobson's self and other developmental considerations and define an array of relatedness possibilities from the least to the most complex along with various considerations of *how relatedness flexibility comes to be limited by experiences at each level of complexity*, i.e. from

(I) the search for connections (Organizing), to

(II) the establishment of reliable channels of mutual attunement (Symbiotic), through separation and individuation to

(III) the firming up of a cohesive sense of self (Selfobject), to

(IV) the highly complex capacity for fully ambivalent triangulated experiences of self and other (Oedipal).

The liberating twist of the Listening Perspectives approach is not to be found simply in the overall reorganization of familiar clinical and developmental concepts along explicitly interpersonal relatedness lines. Rather, *a profound shift of mental organization on the part of the therapeutic therapist is required—a mental shift away from looking for what's "really" there in the person to experiencing what's happening in the here-and-now intersubjective field of mutual and reciprocal influencing.*

From the earliest beginnings of psyche, we can imagine channels being organized on the basis of reciprocal responsiveness between the mothering person's body and personality and the developing infant. We can imagine the "Mommy and me" dance that is forming in the mutual cuing and mutual affective regulatory behaviors being established by the third or fourth month of life. These co-constructed psychological tendrils of mutual relatedness that have been metaphorically termed "symbiosis" by Margaret Mahler (1968) can be thought to evolve according to growing expectations of attuned and misattuned cognitive-affective-conative interactions.[3] In the symbiotic exchange that the infant presumably overlearns, the response of each partner comes to depend upon the response of the other—i.e. mutual affect regulation the neuropsychologists call it (Schore 2004). Peaking by the twelfth to eighteenth month, the symbiotic mutuality, the developing dyadic responsiveness, mutual affect regulation, or forms of symbiotic exchange can all be imagined to remain strong through the twenty-fourth to thirtieth month. Basic character and body structure dates from early in this period as the constitutional and personality variables of the infant come into play with the human relational environment creating the first sense of psychological familiarity and stability. The possible dimensions for construction of the merged dual identity dance of symbiosis are necessarily limited by the foundations of the available connect and disconnect modes that were laid down in the physical and psychical patternings established during the previous Organizing period. The particular emotional and behavioral patterns established in this symbiotic or primary bonding relatedness are thought to follow us throughout our lives (as character structures) as we search for closeness, for intimacy, for security, for familiarity, for physical security, and for love. If some people's stylized search for security and love seems strange, perverse, addictive, or self-abusive, we can only assume that the adult search replicates in some deep emotional way the primary bonding pattern *as the infant and toddler experienced* the symbiotic exchange with his or her caregiving others.

The important aspect of this developmental narrative is not that child development can be demonstrated to proceed in this way, but that such imaginative features can be used in the therapist's mind to search for emotional-relational moves and movements being experienced in the here-and-now therapeutic exchange in order to break through mutual enactments in the transference-countertransference constrictions of the interpersonal field.

This Listening Perspective has been developed for use with what has come to be referred to broadly as "borderline personality organization" and the various "character disorders." (Kernberg 1976; PDM, 2006), and is essentially a way of understanding various aspects of the preverbal interaction patterns that seem to be established during the symbiotic and separating periods of human development. All well-developed people evolved interactional patterns or scenarios related to basic emotional bonding or Symbiotic experience.

I have defined "scenario" as a listening device for highlighting the interactive nature of the early bonding experience as it manifests itself in the replicated or mutually enacted transference-countertransference experience based upon a therapeutic re-creation of relatedness forms, patterns, and modes of the symbiotic periods of both participants that are being mutually enacted. These patterns become replicated in some form when any two people attempt to engage each other emotionally. The (almost "knee-jerk") emotional dance that forms in any emotionally significant relationship can be studied in terms of an interaction, a drama, or set of scenarios that unfold based upon deeply entrenched ways each participant has established for experiencing and relating intimately with others. This Listening Perspective seeks to bring under scrutiny the predominantly preverbal engagement patterns and body configurations that mean attachment, bonding, and love, regardless of what individualized forms those patterns may take. What follows are some case studies to illustrate the listening processes involved when attending to replicated scenarios or mutual enactments that point to symbiotic modes of relating.

Case Study: Jody Messler Davies: "Love in the Afternoon"

I am here reminded of the wonderful case study contributed by Jody Messler Davies, "Love in the Afternoon" (1994). Her client had an intense dread of sexual stimulation in himself, but especially of perceiving arousal in others. At a decisive moment Davies stood against the character scenario of his childhood by telling him that she had indeed had sexual fantasies about him. This precipitated a storm of indignant outrage reminiscent of the frequent storms of outrage the client's mother had frequently directed at him. The client had often recalled how as a boy, following delicious afternoons in mother's bed snuggled up against her body with her reading exciting stories to him, mother would realize that he was in a pleasurable ecstasy intensely enjoying his time with her and then become outraged. Dynamically, mother would seduce the boy with delicious incestuous relating and then when she sensed he was enjoying and feeling aroused by the relating she would become indignant and angrily push him away. Little wonder that he had been totally unable to sustain sexual relationships as an adult. Davies' client had continued to regale her with tantalizing sexual imagery for some time that she had been fending off. But as her analytic curiosity allowed her to consider what this was all about for him she found herself having sexual fantasies and at a critical juncture told him so. His sudden indignant outrage served momentarily to frighten and shame her, replicating how cruelly his mother had raged at and shamed him—and perhaps also signaling his realization that the delicious but perverse scenario with his therapist was crumbling—slowly coming to an end.

In my view her intervention was directly to the point and did serve to bring a long-festering internalized erotic scenario directly under analytic scrutiny. She dared to stand against the scenario by declaring that all of his sexual talk and imagery was indeed having an erotic impact on her whether he wanted to think so or not. Though his instantaneous rage and outrage were momentarily intimidating to Davies, in the confrontation she spoke what the boy's child-self could not speak—that he was stimulating her and that it was both titillating and invasive. And that in raging and shaming her he was attempting to blame her for a mutually stimulating situation that he was deliberately instigating and she was participating in. In role-reversal he had given her in the countertransference the untenable position he had been victim to in childhood. Her speaking up for herself, and therefore against what was happening gave voice to the client's child-self and unmasked the perversity of it all.

Case Study: Lawrence Hedges: "Eros in the Transference"

In my 1991 book *Interpreting the Countertransference* I report on my failed engagement with a woman who, over a three-year period, developed an erotic transference. When I have presented this case to professional audiences therapists regularly protest that the treatment was not a failure, that Dora was very connected to me and that she benefited considerably from our work together. True as this may be, it was the countertransference work that failed because at that time I didn't know how to understand and work with the intense feelings aroused in the erotic transference. I am happy to note that this book achieved recognition as one of the key contributions to psychoanalysis during the centennial celebration of the International Psycho-Analytic

Association in 2009 (Young-Bruehl and Dunbar 2009). Its recognition was undoubtedly due to the theory and technique of relational listening and intervention being advocated here.

At the beginning of hours Dora would sit up and look deeply into my blue eyes, stare at my chest, and enjoy the little hairs that peeped up from my open shirt collar. She would dutifully use the couch for her three times weekly therapy. But at the end of sessions she would again want to breathe deeply and take me in visually—I was her type she said. As the mutual therapeutic seduction progressed there were many elements of mutual enjoyment but Dora continued to fear that I did not like her, that I would see her as a weepy, depressed housewife or find her a pathetic struggling student or some other kind of demeaned creature.

Therapists who have heard or read about our work—usually register sympathy with my plight as all efforts on my part to bring to light the possible meanings of what I experienced as her erotic intrusiveness were impatiently or angrily deflected. Mid-way in treatment I "flinched" (her word) one day when she was adoring me and she went into an immediate angry and anguished tail-spin—wildly declaring that I had never loved her, that I truly did think all the negative things about her that she feared I did, that she could never trust me again, that she must stop her therapy at once. I recovered momentarily and convinced her to keep working, which we did for another year before a similar incident occurred and she abruptly terminated—a painful experience for both of us.

I had been, almost from the outset, struggling with feeling intruded upon by her ongoing erotic interest in me and had sought consultation which did put me in touch with childhood material of my own that related to my experience of a sexually intrusive adopted sister and a highly intrusive seductive mother.

One interesting feature of this vignette, which is common to a number of replication/counter-replication engagements, is the sexualization of the therapeutic relationship. While sexualization may take various forms and be attributed to different causes, a few common themes often emerge.

One frequent determinant for the sexualization of the dyadic experience is the fusion or confusion between affection and sexuality. That is, certain kinds of sensual and/or affectionate attachments from early childhood are retained in the personality through puberty when they become enmeshed in an individual's sexuality. The sexualized affection is then transferred to all or to certain subsequent relationships including the therapeutic one.

Another cause for sexualization of replicated interactions arises from the ways in which body-mind-relationship boundaries form or fail to form fully in early childhood relationships. In various ways, body-mind-relationship boundaries may remain defined idiosyncratically and, to a greater or lesser extent, imbued with erotic or incestuous overtones. Early ego functions surrounding issues of interpersonal boundary definition may have been limited or peculiar for a variety of reasons. The result is that later sexual development does not become integrated smoothly into conventional definitions of interpersonal boundaries and certain merger experiences may remain erotized.

In the present vignette a third possibility to account for the sexualization of the replication arises which is different from those ordinarily encountered. Here *the sexualized replicated transference shows up as function of the therapist's personal vulnerabilities or sensitivities* which would not need to be at all sexual in nature. That is, when a symbiotic or separating dyadic exchange is replicated in the analytic relationship, it is the affective mode of relatedness that is reestablished on a pre- or non-verbal basis. The content of the interaction is often not of particular interest in itself, but *what is of crucial importance is the affective nature of the emotional interchange to be replicated.*

What had to be replicated with Dora was a particular style, pattern or model of early mother-child relatedness in which the child felt that whole sectors of her spontaneous and creative potentials had to be suppressed in order to support mother's vulnerable personality functioning. Mother's dependency hung heavily on this child as she demanded incessant reassurances in a variety of ways leaving the girl feeling elated that her mother loved her and simultaneously helpless and stifled by her mother's intrusive attention which was so totally fixed on her in order to maintain mother's cohesiveness and functioning in the world.

Dora had derived much enjoyment and satisfaction from what she experienced as my permission to let her gaze at me and to feel consolidated as a result of her erotically tinged scrutiny of my eyes, my hair, my chest and other parts of my body. So far as I could determine there was no history of overt incest in her family though her older brother was frequently obnoxious using double entendres with "off color" implications. So I would have to surmise that *she was very skillful in ferreting out an aspect of my personality which was vulnerable to a similar quality of emotional threat which her early relationship with her mother and possibly also an insinuating brother contained.*

My assuming that the problem was created by a series of episodes in *my* preadolescence or a personal vulnerability in *my* personality dating to my own symbiosis, ignored completely the possibility that this vulnerability was being actively stimulated by her at a level not conscious to either of us *for the purposes of recreating a certain stylized and highly charged emotional atmosphere.* In considering the countertransference material in the narrow sense and acknowledging a specific vulnerability in my historical past, I failed to appreciate the transference replication the mutual enactments involved. I thereby lost the opportunity to move the consideration of the transference replication of uneasiness, fear, hatred, confinement, and strangulated creativity, which I was feeling onto the plane of the therapy. It was not until several years later that I came to understand where I had gone wrong. The process of countertransference interpretation is subject to considerable "give and take" creative interaction between two people and often takes months of collaborative work to accomplish. In replication or mutual enactment the unique personality features of the therapist are utilized for expressive purposes by the client. The relevant dimensions can be expected to become embedded in or entangled with the personal images and idioms peculiar to the therapist's personality or character.

Three Common Treatment Errors

In attempting to analyze replicated symbiotic or merger scenarios, three technical errors commonly arise in regard to handling the countertransference.

The first and perhaps most widely noted error is the therapist's simply ignoring disturbing countertransference feelings because he or she knows them to be related to recurring personal issues or sensitivities.

The second widespread technical error is the therapist's disregard of probable countertransference distortions or idiomatic biases in favor of getting some "fix" on what is "really happening"—perhaps in the form of a theoretical notion borrowed from or confirmed by a well-known authority regarding "defensiveness," "splitting," "narcissistic rage," "incestuous entanglements," "empathic failure," "emerging archetypes," or whatever.

The report I have offered of my countertransference entanglement with Dora illustrates yet a third variety of technical error—a readiness on the therapist's part to assume personal responsibility for the emerging disruption or untoward feelings, thereby sidestepping completely the more important interactional/communicational component of mutual enactment which contains the crucial processes and imagos required for the psychoanalytic therapy, the emergence of which two people are resisting.

Having by now had the opportunity as a supervisor as well as in subsequent consulting work of my own to learn how to identify broadly and to launch into collaborative work on specifics of this kind of countertransference entanglement, I have been able when reviewing the present case to have a confident sense of the right general direction the work might have taken and did not. I'm sure if I had understood what we were dealing with I could have found some tactful way to tell Dora that I did not like the erotic interest she was taking in me. First, because it stimulated uncomfortable feelings from my own past. But more importantly, because it seemed to me she was needing to put me in the untenable position she felt in as a child with her mother's intrusiveness and we weren't really looking at what was important. We had mutually created in the enactments dissociated aspects of each of ourselves.

Case Study: Stephen Mitchell: The Horror of Surrendering

Freud (1937) taught us that for a man to take in something from another man is psychically equivalent to surrendering to homoerotic longings, femininity, and the loss of male potency. But Mitchell points out from our modern point of view that perhaps all men in one way or another long to be liberated from the burdens of socially constructed male-gendered identity (1997).

To illustrate this thesis Mitchell recounts an analysis he conducted with an artist who had gotten into a stalemate after seven years with his former analyst. Gender lines were tightly drawn in the client's family of origin. His father was a self-absorbed artist whose ambitions were greater than his talents. His mother had become embittered by his father's passivity and isolation and divorced him when the client was ten. He became closely aligned with his father because of his mother's hatred of all men but even so his father hardly saw him. Mitchell's client fantasized both he and his father to be superior, suffering and unrecognized geniuses. Although the son was a promising artist, much more successful than his father, he had a habit of sabotaging himself as if actively succeeding were somehow terrifying. He constantly sought leads and advice from others including his analyst about what he should do and how he should spend his time. He valued more than anything else what someone else could bring or give to him. In sexual intercourse, he reported at times feeling confusion over whether the aroused penis was his or the woman's. He was excited by the thought of what being penetrated by a penis might feel like.

The transference in both analyses was organized around the desire and dread of what he could get from the analysts, both men. The analysts were both seen as possessing precious knowledge that they sadistically withheld. He had read some things Mitchell had written and felt that he would be more interactive than the previous analyst, would give him more. But he was soon struck with how insightful the writings had been and how dull Mitchell seemed as an analyst in person.

What seemed not to have come out in the previous work was what a desolate image of masculinity this man had inherited from his father—an identity that condemned him to live in a depressive heroic solitude. His longing to be penetrated—by ideas, by a penis, by scintillating analytic interpretations—represented "both a desperate hope finally to get something from his father and an escape from the masculine confinement that constituted being a man. (p. 251)"

In the transference Mitchell is granted superior knowledge making the client dependent on getting the analyst to deliver or else suffering from deprivation. Early on he had a hard time remembering anything Mitchell said but finally fixated on one of the analyst's questions. In speaking of his last analysis he lamented that for him to change he would have to give up a sense of himself as special—which he wasn't sure he could ever do. Mitchell asked where he got the sense that the major factor in constructive change would entail his giving up something very precious to him. The question served to define a different kind of relationship that existed with Mitchell which didn't demand submission.

> The first analyst seemed to be saying something like, "Your problems with assertiveness are due to your remaining your very special father's very special little girl. Cut it out; give all that up." Yet the patient experienced that injunction as implicitly claiming, "My penis/authority is bigger and better than your father's. I want you as my little girl. To make it with me, you have to give up him." (p. 252)

Gradually in the role-reversal countertransference Mitchell found himself implicitly or explicitly making such submissive claims himself:

> an envy of his relationship with his father,…seductive hints that he could certainly be a most loyal and rewarding devotee, if only I could convince him I had the right stuff; an intellectual toughness and competitiveness in him that made it clear that, if I was not man enough to make him want to be my little girl, he would certainly make me his; an admiration for his intellectual prowess and vast knowledge of things I was interested in that made a passive surrender to him both tempting and dangerous; and so on. (p. 252)

Using this case example, Mitchell holds the opinion that for contemporary analysts the decisive arena for working on gender and gender identification issues is in the complex interpersonal negotiations of the analytic relationship.

> This man needed to realize that he had co-created the impasse in his first analysis…with his horror of a surrender, which he also deeply longed for. Our joint task was to find a way for us to engage each other by which we could alternately give and receive, alternately exert power and be vitalized by the prowess of the other, and simultaneously lessen the threat of self-betrayal and humiliation (p. 252).

The Symbiotic Replicated Transference-Countertransference

Self and other configurations or constrictions thought to originate in the symbiotic period of relatedness human development are secured for analysis through the replicated or mutually enacted transference-countertransference (Hedges 1983, 1992). Writers such as Winnicott, Ferenczi, and Balint have held that special provision needs to be made in the analytic relationship for these earlier relational issues to be seen and analyzed. Following Blanck and Blanck (1979), I speak of the transferences from this early period of development as more than mere transfer of instinctual feelings from oedipal parents (Hedges 1983). Symbiotic or early bonding experiences presumably occurred at a time in the client's life when infant and caregiver engaged in a mutual cuing or affect regulation process in which two lived and experienced each other in many ways as one. The replicating transference-countertransference can be expected to be a reliving at an unconscious or preconscious emotional level of patterns, styles, and modes of relatedness once known in relation to the mutually affect-relating symbiotic (m)other. In the original symbiosis, the (m)other is hooked by the power of the relatedness. In replication, the analyst must be equally hooked at a preverbal emotional level for the nature of the bond to begin to become apparent. Mutual affect regulation and interpersonal enactments comprise the replicating transference-countertransference matrix.

Frequently in case conferences I hear a therapist making remarks such as: "I am going to present this case because somehow I find myself doing things I don't ordinarily do in my practice." Or, "This person has a way of manipulating me that I find upsetting." Or, "I feel like I'm being set up for something, that something isn't right, that I don't know what's going on with this person, that somehow I am being duped." Such expressions register the sense of interpersonal boundaries being tapped or stretched from the therapist's ordinarily expectable personal and/or professional guidelines and limits. Studying how the therapist experiences these boundary demands, crossings, or violations begins to give clues to the preverbal emotional replication being lived out in the therapeutic interaction by both parties.

Another way of thinking about this is to say that the Client has the project of attempting to communicate preverbal memories to the therapist. In doing so he or she tends to ferret out and use various aspects of the analyst's personal responsiveness for the purpose of arranging an emotional replication or mutual enactment of the way things once were. To the therapist it often feels as though his or her Achilles' heel has been found, that the client has learned how to " push my buttons." That is, the earliest bond, the first love, and the foundational realities of our lives are derived from the assumptions we make about the environment and important people in it. This set of attitudes, beliefs, assumptions, and relatedness modes becomes so firmly entrenched that all intimate relationships can be expected to touch upon how we experience the world through symbiotic templates. The merged sense we have regarding how intimate relationships "should" be is so automatic and entrenched as to be readily confused with reality. A very definite set of expectations and relatedness difficulties arises and the client is loudly or even silently adamant in the insistence that such and such is the way things must go between us. *An adversarial atmosphere arises* (Stern, in press). Gradually the analytic therapist feels closed in on all sides or backed into a corner until he or she can find a way to make an effective relational intervention; a way to "stand against the scenario" (Hedges 1983). The resistance is often so severe as to make relinquishing of the sought-for patterns almost an impossibility.

Therapy with Symbiotic Relatedness Scenarios

The first problem in therapy with people experiencing borderline level relating is for the therapist to be able to place the difficulties in an interactive, symbiotic format so that exactly what the relatedness demand is comes into bold relief. Not only is this a cognitive task involving problem-solving with new ideas, but the emotional relatedness dimension itself necessarily has engaged the therapist in many unconscious or automatic enactments so that the therapist's own character defenses become activated. But even when a therapist is skilled enough to be able to see the relatedness dimension insisted on by the client, and even when the defensive structure of the therapist can be more or less laid aside for the moment, making verbal interpretations of complex nonverbal experiences poses an entirely new set of impossible problems. Therapists have been known to talk themselves blue in the face and what they were saying was well formulated but somehow it still didn't hit the mark. The client might even agree, even cognitively elaborate the therapist's ideas, or make behavioral changes in accordance with the interpretations, but still there is no connection to the deep, nonverbal emotional layers that the interactive dilemma springs from. *Verbal interpretations of preverbal symbiotic relatedness patterns are not effective until the issues are in active replication (mutual enactment) in the analytic relationship or in a parallel relationship and unless the interpretation functions as some sort of active confrontation of the relatedness mode in here-and-now relating.*

"Confrontation" is used here cautiously, and does not mean that the person or behavior is being confronted, but rather, the forms, modes, or patterns of constricted relating that arise from experiencing emotional relatedness templates from the Symbiotic past are the object of the transference or enactment confrontation. Furthermore, it may be the client who first has the "new perception" that leads to dissolution of the enactment (Stern, 2010). Since the Symbiosis is thought to consist of a set of stylized relatedness patterns and modes that cannot be spoken, if they are ever to become known they will manifest themselves in the non- or para-verbal exchanges between two people. Bromberg (2011) and Stern (2010) make clear that those enactments must *actually* occur before it is possible to know them or to formulate them into words. As the exchange proceeds, a pattern of relating will emerge with regular expectations of how therapist and client are to interact under varying conditions. These patterns are frequently referred to as "replications" or "enactments". The subjective "Mommy and me are one" dimension becomes inadvertently or unwittingly lived out in the exchange, beginning with the dependency or care aspects implicit in the therapeutic situation. By looking for a recurring pattern or scenario that is regularly a part of the dyadic relatedness, the therapist becomes aware that the symbiotic or "Mommy and me" interaction pattern gradually appears in each of its particulars as it is lived out in relatedness expectations. Too rigid or too loose boundaries on the part of the therapist may thwart the process. Unlike the study of neurosis, in which a series of rules or policies (the frame) are established to bring the neurotic longings sharply in focus for verbal-symbolic interpretation, the study of symbiosis requires that the therapist maintain whatever minimal limits and boundaries are needed to preserve personal and professional integrity, and then watch to see how the client chooses to structure the relatedness and attempts to play with, stretch, or attempts to violate what might otherwise be considered interpersonal boundaries. What can then be observed and opened to comment are the idiosyncratic ways in which the relationship becomes oriented and structured by the needs and demands of both therapist and client. That is, the replicated transference-countertransference enactments can be expected to be nonverbal and interactional in their impact, a silent development in the spontaneous relating of two human beings. A great deal of talk or chatter may occur as the therapist attempts to inquire and offer ideas, but the crucial event of transformation will not occur as a result of verbal work *per se*, but rather or a result of non- or para-verbal action, interaction, or enactment that may or may not later be formulated (Stern, in press).

Passive and Active Transference-Countertransference Enactments

Two major forms of the replication or enactment are to be watched for: the passive version and the active version. The passive replication, though often unnoticed for long periods, is the experience in the transference of the therapist and the listening situation in some particular way like the preverbal interaction with an early caregiver. For example, the demand for a certain fee, or for regular and timely appointments becomes experienced like some demand from a symbiotic parent for time and energy to be directed not as the infant/client would have it but as the parent/therapist insists.

Countertransference studies have led to consideration of active replication of the symbiotic dimension in which a role reversal is entailed. That is, the client is "doing unto the therapist what was once done unto him." That is, a position of passive weakness or trauma is turned into active victory in the role reversal. The client acts in place of the parent, foisting onto the therapist relatedness demands that the client once experienced as being foisted upon him or her. An array of reactions might emerge in either participant of the passive replication: irritation, injury, rage, spite, excitement, rebellion, conformity, lust, etc.—each would represent the revival of some emotional relatedness mode from early childhood. Speaking or interpreting these things is often welcome and well received but typically goes nowhere. In the replicated transference, in the passive or active forms, a certain emotional climate is set up by the client and the therapist is expected to be in agreement or to conform to it. So long as the therapist is living his or her part well, things go well. But when the therapist fails to obey (inadvertently or through active confrontation of the scenario) the relatedness rules that have been laid down, a disturbance in the relationship ensues. This splitting of good and bad affective experiences keeps the therapist on target in understanding the exact nature of the relatedness hopes and expectations under study.

Freud's (1915) formulation is that of turning passive trauma into active victory. Anna Freud's (1937) formulation is "identification with the aggressor." Her interpretation rests on the truism that no matter how good the parenting process, the parental ministration is frequently experienced by the infant as an aggressive intrusion into his or her space for instinctual expression. Klein (1946) formulates in terms of "projective identification," noting that early incorporated "bad objects" are made available for analysis by projection into the person of the analyst.

Alice Balint (1943), in a brilliant tour de force, has detailed the process of primary identification and holds that we identify with what cannot be readily used and incorporated into the nurturing process. That is, it is the negative, the overwhelming or traumatic, that poses a problem for the infant. In primary identification as the infant attempts to solve the problem of negative intrusions, she or he builds a mental model of the parental emotional response to be understood because it is troublesome or intrusive. As the early model is built, it becomes a foundational part of the early structure of the child's mind. In active replication transferences these living modes based on primary identification emerge with clarity in the analytic interactions.

In addressing a group of Superior Court judges and mediators involved in child custody decisions regarding the subject of projections encountered in their work, I once spoke of "reciprocal scripting." Most everyone these days understands the notion of scripting—that we each have an emotional life script that we manage to live out again and again in different situations. With vignettes from therapy and extrapolations into parents fighting for custody of their children, I was able to demonstrate what sitting ducks mediators and judges are to being snared into these reciprocal scripts by parents and attorneys, into knee-jerk responses and judgments which may have nothing to do with the task at hand of acting in the best interests of the child (Hedges 1994d). But the fresh twist in "reciprocal scripting" is to learn that our life script also contains exactly what the other person is to say or do in response to us. That is, not only is each of us locked into endlessly repeating patterns of personal relating, but we are equally locked into finding, creating, or stimulating circumstances in which how the other person is supposed to relate or respond is also unwittingly scripted by us. We tend to "do unto others what was done unto us." A scenario, thus constructed from observing the emotional exchange between client and therapist, is not expected to be an exact recreation of historical truth as it might have been viewed objectively at the time. Rather, the interactional patterns that become discerned, defined, enacted and perceived produce emotional-interactional truth. These relational scripts reflect the internal experience of the infant as recorded in the body and the style of affect engagement with others, rather than actual memories of any real or discrete events.

The pictures, affects, and words that emerge as a joint creation of the two participants serve to define real experiences of some sort and are often cast into a language of metaphoric reconstruction of past reality. Often a client will wonder if such and such an event that seems so true or is becoming so vivid in memory ever really happened. It does little good to speculate about the veracity of the memory *per se* and certainly trusting the therapist's gut level belief that it really did happen cannot be safe since so much transference and countertransference is being evoked at such times. There can be no doubt that seductions and abuses are widespread and that, whether or not a particular event can be depicted as happening on a particular date in history, a violation or series of seductive intrusions did occur, even if only in the overall atmosphere of caregiving that existed at the time. But of much greater importance than the actual veracity of a certain seduction or abuse, is the question of how that seduction or abuse is being replicated in the here-and-now transference-countertransference engagement.

Replicating transference-countertransference enactments are bound to develop with all people who have been fortunate enough to have experienced a symbiosis and who have developed the capacity for affective relatedness. The question in a therapeutic process is when and how it will reappear and what will the therapist have done or failed to do to facilitate its emergence. That is, when the "bad child" is being projected into us, when the aggressive parent imago seeks to attack or limit us, when we are the passive target for the victorious identificatory aggressions and seductions from the client's infantile history—how then do we receive and attempt to define the intrusions, the abuses, the identifications and projections that were once experienced? Moreover, how do we find words to begin capturing the countertransference experience and enactment as a result of a successful role-reversal replication or mutual enactment of symbiotic patterns? Once again the parent-child metaphors will come to our rescue when trying to form pictures to depict what it feels like to be limited, abused, provoked, teased, tantalized, argued with, seduced, and so forth.

But even if we have been more or less successful in fixing on crucial aspects of projected replication experiences and putting our experiences into words and pictures for ourselves, we face once again the problem of how to communicate our understandings so that the client can make use of them for transformational purposes. Whether the aspect of the countertransference we are trying to bring to light is the passive or active replication, we repeatedly find that in trying to put preverbal affective experience that has a quality of relational reality into pictures, scenes, and words that might define that experience, our words often either fail or fall on deaf ears. Stern has expressed this in terms of not only "unformulated experience" but "non-verbal experience" (Stern, in press) Therapists often liken it to a mother speaking to an infant, explaining complicated things that the infant has no way of grasping. The infant may listen intently, study mother's face and the sounds of her voice, and respond in a variety of ways, but the verbal understanding cannot be received. Likewise the infant studies carefully Mother's face and body for experiences she is having that she perceives but cannot formulate. Kohut declares that a self develops because a mother addresses the child from the first day of life as though the child had a self. We need to keep in mind that many of our verbalizations are to keep ourselves oriented to the task at hand and while they may be received in many ways may not yet be comprehensible to the client. Bollas (1987) holds that finding creative ways of speaking the countertransference is tantamount to putting words on preverbal experience that the client cannot at present verbalize. Speaking the countertransference represents interpreting the early mother-child idiom of being and relating (Hedges 1983, 1992).

Resistance to Relinquishing Symbiotic Modes

Perhaps the most difficult resistance at this level is to seeing the destructive and masochistic aspects of the replication in such a way that the person feels impelled to relinquish the relatedness modes that form the core of his or her identity, the relatedness memories that have come to spell love, or mother, or safety, or familiarity. The symbiotic relatedness modes are so foundational to the way we organize and orient our entire beings that a wholesale shift in lifestyle and interpersonal relatedness will be required if we wish to experience greater relational freedom. People are not only reluctant but terrified to give up ways of being that are basic to how they experience reality. The cry of resistance is always heard in one form or another, "I can't do it, you must do it for me!" It can take many forms: "I can't change without a completely safe relationship." "Unless I can be held and allowed complete internal integration of my true self I can't possibility develop." "Your style of working or personality simply will not allow me to do what I must do. I need a therapist who…" The bottom line is "I can't (or won't) give it up." Clients do not want to hear the interpretation of active and passive scenarios because it would mean having to give up a way of relating dependently, safely, or familiarly with a (longed-for or fantasized) maternal object who could be relied on for an expectable set of responses—be they good or bad. We encountered this earlier in the Davies case study where her client did his best to shame her into capitulation. To relinquish long-held ways of relating is tantamount to giving up our mother, letting her die, of being without our main ways of greeting the world. No wonder no one wants to individuate; it means a crumbling of ego function that was built on the old tried and true symbiotic modes of relating. Relinquishing old symbiotic/character modes necessarily produces tremendous disruption, disorientation, and grief that our stable modes of relating are collapsing and that we are fragmenting, losing our footing, loosening our grip on what we once thought was real. I have observed the most painful and horrendous regressions in the service of therapeutic progress when Symbiotic and/or Organizing modes are relinquished. More than once I have heard a person say, "Where is my old self? I used to be able to function even though I was screwed up," or "If I'd known how painful and disorganizing this process would be I don't know if I would have started." I have watched many therapeutic processes abort just on the brink of a major relinquishing of symbiotic relating—under some form of the guise "You must do it for me," or "I must feel good and you must provide those feelings for me."

Sometimes client and therapist find ways of rationalizing the failure and cheering each other up with a Hollywood sunset termination. Preferable to me is the greater honesty inherent when both end up feeling defeated that they have tried their best to make it safe for the fragmenting loss to occur, but as the Organizing or psychotic aspects underneath are activated, the fears are too strong or the reality consequences at the time are too great for one or the other or both to continue the therapy. In principle, *I believe the relinquishing as well as a working through of the psychotic or Organizing aspects of personality is always possible.* But in practice we have to consider the personal resources available to the client as well as the therapist at the time, the strength of the conditioning factors as originally laid down, and the analyst's preparedness to experience Organizing regressions that a crumbling of symbiotic structures in the client are likely to stimulate. I was interested in how Heinz Kohut (1984) expressed this possibility:

In the psychoses, including those covertly psychotic personality organizations (central hollowness, but a well-developed peripheral layer of defensive structures) for which I reserve the term borderline states, a nuclear self has not been shaped in early development. ... In these cases the psychoanalytic situation [as classically conceived] does not bring about the long-term activation of the central chaos of the self within a workable transference that is a precondition for setting in motion the processes that would lead to the creation, *de novo,* of a nuclear self. In order to lead to a causal cure, the therapeutic process would have to penetrate beneath the organized layers—the defensive structures—of the patient's self and permit the prolonged reexperiencing of oscillations between prepsychological chaos and the security provided by primitive merger with an archaic selfobject. *It is certainly imaginable that, even in adult life, the repeated experience of optimal frustration in an archaic homeostatic selfobject environment brought about in the analytic situation would lead,as in earliest infancy, to the birth of a nuclear self.* (p. 8, italics added).

Kohut acknowledges that in expressing reservations about the analyzability of prespychological states, he may be expressing his own personal limits as a psychoanalyst. As a diagnostic relativist, Kohut defines the categories of psychosis and borderline as states of prepsychological chaos, which the empathic instruments of the psychoanalytic observer as traditionally conceived would be unable to comprehend. But Kohut acknowledges that the basis for his conviction may be his personal fear that in following a person empathically into prepsychological territory he would not be able to hold the empathic bond when the basic transference emerges and the person for protracted periods of time would have to "borrow the analyst's personality in order to survive" (p. 9). Thirty years later the scope of psychotherapy has certainly expanded to include treatment of borderline and psychotic personality features in much the same way that Kohut envisions.

Responding to the Negative Therapeutic Reactions

Freud's discussions of "negative therapeutic reactions" rest upon lifelong dependence, on overidealization, and on a penchant for moral masochism that the continued living out of the character scenario gratifies. And so the person on the threshold of cure abruptly aborts the therapeutic process, often disillusioned or enraged with the therapist (Freud 1923,1924a, 1932).

The interpretive response to the insistence that "you must do it for me" is based on an understanding of how ego advances are accomplished in general but prototypically during the symbiosis when so many skills are being learned. Everyone learns for another. Children learn for mother and later for teachers, for love, and finally for the love involved in self-esteem. But mother's presence is initially required for venturing out at the symbiotic level. Likewise in some way *the real emotional presence of the therapist* in a supportive and reinforcing way is required at the point that a scenario is being relinquished. This is not the kind of support referred to in supportive psychotherapy, a giving up on the analyzability of something or someone. Nor is this support focused at the level of behavior, or adjustment, or getting better *per se*. The active and supportive intervention needs to be conceived as a "Mommy and me" togetherness project like learning to walk, to tie shoes, to draw, or later to ride a bike or to write. All people resist vigorously giving up their earliest and most foundational love bond in whatever form its memory is retained. And when it begins to crumble, suicidal and death fears abound that are properly interpreted as "Indeed, you are dying; the only self you have ever known is being killed off by what you are accomplishing in therapy." Relinquishing symbiotic modes is also equivalent to severing the maternal bond, to killing off the emotional presence of the internalized mother. "You are afraid because there is nothing in your life experience to suggest that things will ever be any different." The following case illustrates how the therapist replicates the scenario then after a new perception of what's going on finds a way to "stand against" the scenario.

Case Study: Sarah Turner-Miller: 'Night, Mother

Bioenergetic therapist Sarah Turner-Miller recounts a year-long saga with her client, Maggie, whom she describes as a middle-aged woman, groomed but untidy with a worn, thrift-store look. Her large eyes not only stare but seem to look completely through Sarah. Clutching her purse she declares that therapy is her last stop. She tells Sarah that she is agitated and cannot sleep; that she feels ugly like she does not belong on earth, like she doesn't exist.

Maggie was adopted at 4 months of age. Her adoptive parents had two older sons. Maggie bonded with her father, who died when she was 10. Mother remarried and her new husband had a son who had sex in the afternoon with different people and masturbated in front of her. She received no protection. "My mother is like a black apple. I feel pain and darkness—no hope. Why bother? I'm tired. Nothing works."

Sarah struggles to establish a connection with Maggie. Every now and then she sees a flash in Maggie's eyes that acknowledges that she is there. Sarah feels morbid when she is with Maggie, craving rest and sun. She feels she is with a person who is already dead as if Sarah has to provide meaningful existence for both of them.

Maggie clearly craves some kind of sustained connection, some symbiotic tie, with Sarah even though paradoxically it seems somehow life-threatening to her. Maggie unconsciously knows her limited experience of symbiosis to be so destructive that she loses either way—with or without connection. She wants Sarah to be a successful mother to her and to pull her from her deep schizoid withdrawal.

Sarah experiences Maggie as filling the room with a hostile oozing energy that is full of vile hatred. Sarah finds herself thinking: "I hate you! I hate you! Go away—disappear—don't kill yourself; just get out of my space. The countertransference is so pervasive and persistent that Sarah can hardly breathe, but now she knows how hated Maggie was. Says Sarah: "She needs to know I know, to feel that I have some sense of how hated she was. She needs to hear that I mourn her lost humanity and that I cringe at her deadening processes."

The countertransference needs to somehow be spoken. Sarah hesitatingly begins,

> I have some very important things to share with you today. These are feelings, thoughts, observations about myself when I'm with you that may help us understand your difficulties even more....What happened to you was so early in your life there is no way for you to tell me just how terrible you feel. There is only the therapeutic dance that goes on between us for you to show me what goes on deep inside of you....As we get to know one another I essentially become, in psychic experience, you the infant and you become your parents. Thus I come to know your experience

110

by living out your inner life. ...Often and from the very beginning, I have experience intense feelings that do not seem to be mine. I feel scared and confused around you. I feel I am not enough for you—that there is some awesome rage and chaos that I can't get out of easily. I feel depleted, drained of my life. I feel evil. ...When I try to connect with you, I feel destroyed in my efforts. We know this is not your intention; not you, consciously. You are showing me something important. (pp 130-131)

Maggie seemed somewhat dazed by this session and I checked on her later by phone. The next session Maggie brought in two watercolor paintings that she said were provoked by our last meeting. One was a pregnant woman painted black with a fetus of blue with a red center. The other was a design with a dark center. She said, "This is what it's like to be in the black hole. It starts at the center and bleeds out, the black hole contains it, controls it, and won't let it live....I know you know something about us and I feel calmer."

Next Maggie brought Sarah her "bad stuff" in a brown paper bag. Bad stuff refers to her favorite morbid movies, but she explains that she has left the most important one at home. Shortly Maggie phones Sarah to tell her that she wants to kill herself and believes she can. Sarah convinces her to go to her trusted gynecologist and he got her to a psychiatrist who prescribed Prozac and Xanax.

Maggie then brings her favorite video, 'Night, Mother, for safekeeping in Sarah's office. 'Night, Mother is a play by Marsha Norman that probes deeply into a mother-daughter symbiosis that ends in a suicide dance of the deepest despair and loneliness.

Maggie happens upon the movie which becomes her transitional object. She has watched it hundreds of times. The interaction between daughter Jessie and her Mama has struck a deep place within Maggie. She, like Jessie, wishes to die and knows that her life as she lives it has to end. She is morbidly invested in every word. She wants Sarah to join in.

The movie portrays the evening in which Jessie tells her mother she is going to kill herself that night. We follow the two through gripping conversations in which painful aspects of Jessie's life, including her struggle with epilepsy, are worked over by the two. Jessie hurriedly rushes down the hall with Mama following screaming and banging on the locked door until the fatal gunshot is heard. "Jessie, Jessie, child ... Forgive me. (Pause) I thought you were mine."

Maggie wants Sarah to play *'Night, Mother* with her. Watching the movie and reading the script has enlightened Sarah about the nature of the transference-countertransference matrix she has felt so desperately caught up into.

> I feel like I've been struck in the head by lightning bolts. She carries the video around in a paper bag. She leaves it in my office for safekeeping with a great deal of pomp and circumstance. She tells me that as long as I have *'Night, Mother* in my possession, she won't do anything to hurt herself. She promises to leave it with me for so many weeks, then asks for it in the next session. Keep this dangerous movie away from me, she begs and then sneers at me and insists on having it back that instant! In spite of the rich material we discuss at length, the obsession exhausts us both. (p.136)

Finally Sarah has had enough:

> I've had it with this *'Night, Mother* spook show. I hate feeling responsible for keeping Maggie alive, as if I could. I know the agony of Mama. It's my turn to let her know how much I detest being in this position. The dialogue from that session went like this: "I can't be warm and caring when you turn me into a hospital or police person whose job is to keep you from killing yourself. I don't want that job! Your most important way to relate to life is in the *'Night, Mother* game. I cannot play it with you. I will not be your "'Night, Mother." It's not right for me. You've got to stop this! When you endanger your life, you can't have me....Jessie had the last word with Mama, the blast of a gun. I know you're looking for a way to have the last word with me....I really want to relate to you. We can connect in a real way; as two warm loving humans. (p. 136)

Maggie says somehow our last session when "You blew up at me" helped her to get some things into a new perspective, that she could feel Sarah better. She watched *'Night, Mother* again....This time she saw a girl who had lived a lifetime of pain that she never expressed to anyone and how no one picked up on her pain, so they thought everything was fine. She also saw someone who was already dead basically; that killing herself was just the completion of the physical act of something that had long been dead.

She tells Sarah that she now knows that Sarah understands. That Jesse is someone who had been hurt all her life, yet had not given voice to that pain until that one evening when it all came out. Maggie told Sarah that she now understands why she identifies so much with

113

that movie. She's going to read the script again to see if she can experience it from a different perspective.

Maggie shortly reports feeling more balanced. She even smiles at Sarah now. Maggie says she almost trusts Sarah, that she can see the craziness of *'Night, Mother* and how she used to feel a victim of it. She dreams, "I asked you what do you think of your daughter? You said, 'I couldn't do without her. She's so good.'"

Soon Maggie wants a clean break from therapy so the two went through several months of termination. Maggie has no money and Sarah has been carrying a bill up to $5,000 because Maggie needed the therapy and because Sarah has feared for her life.

Two months after termination Maggie filed for bankruptcy, her whereabouts unknown.

Sarah:

> It's as if the therapy was her birthright—that she shouldn't have to pay to exist in my office. What she owed me is really what was owed to her in nature a thousand times over: a real mother with goodness and love. Emotional bankruptcy was filed on her a long time ago. She played it out to the bitter end. From the position Maggie left me in I can now say, knowing what it means to her, "Good night, Mother." But at least it is I who am symbolically left for dead and she, as survivor, is on her own to find her way in the world.

> Wherever Maggie is, I wish her well. (p. 139)

In this therapy we witness the replication of the two participants' symbiotic scenarios until Sarah has a "new perception" of their mutual

114

enactments of dissociated aspects of themselves (Stern 2010). At that point Sarah retrieves her dissociated anger and "stands against" the symbiotic enactments, thus giving both a new degree of "relatedness flexibility" (Hedges 2013c,d) or "relational freedom" (Stern, in press).

Case Study: Donnel Stern: "Perhaps you should have called me."

I had the rare opportunity and pleasure to respond to a case presentation given at the Newport Psychoanalytic Institute on March 16, 2013 by Donnel Stern. The case of William is to appear in his "Relational Freedom" chapter of his forthcoming book (in press). Here are my remarks on the case that relate to the problem of confrontation and relinquishment of Symbiotic enactments.

Don, let's examine the material you have presented in your work with William, searching, as always, for transference and countertransference themes, dissociations, and enactments that might be limiting his and/or your relatedness flexibility or, in your terms, relational freedom.

Over the time you have spent with William he tells you about and enacts with you his "symbiotic false self compliance scenario" learned in relation to a self-centered mother who expects to be mirrored in her narcissistic grandiosity by his appreciation and gratitude—though his compliance is fraught with bitter resentment. This early symbiotic mode or scenario was transferred—not necessarily inappropriately—by William onto his equally, we are told, narcissistic father.

"Symbiotic scenario" is a term coined in this particular Listening Perspective to denote the *internalized relational template* or *implicit object relations fantasy* operative at this preverbal level of awareness and being *"replicated"—actually lived out or enacted in emotionally significant relationships, including the transference-countertransference intersubjective field* (Hedges 1983, 1992, 2005).

Through a role-reversal—one endemic to replicated symbiotic relational templates or scenarios—William insists on selfobject appreciation and gratitude from his wife as well as his analyst, (and, like his own parents, no doubt in muted ways from his own three children). But unlike what we expect in the Selfobject listening perspective William is unable to benefit from empathic mirroring either from his wife Jan or you. Rather, William's family and analyst are compulsively assigned the reciprocal role from his family of origin of remaining emotionally distant or standoffish.

Other features of the symbiotic listening perspective discernible in the material presented include (1) the splitting of affects when compliance with the scenario is or is not being achieved in the transference; (2) chronic limitations in ego capacities—in William's case debilitating anxieties in the area of social and romantic relations; and (3) personal identity development that is limited largely to work-related preoccupations.

And so Don, you welcome and engage William and you two await the expectable, necessarily unconscious, split off, dissociated aspects of transference-countertransference replications as they fall into place. Over time the analyst and patient alert each other to experiencing and then to the perceiving of various aspects of their replicated interactional scenarios.

As you have so well observed, it's only a matter of time before an adversarial emotional atmosphere develops in the interpersonal field at the symbiotic level of relatedness complexity. "What's going on here anyway? Something is wrong here; something must be done to straighten matters out." For this reason, I have spoken of countertransference as the "royal road to understanding the symbiotic replication experience" (1983, 1992).

First, as therapists we find ourselves in the role of the early parents—some aspect of our analytic relatedness subtly *replicates or re-enacts* the damaging influences known in early childhood. But then we also find ourselves in a role-reversal—experiencing in the countertransference the emotional life of the infant self of our patient, passively experiencing the misattunement and abuse foisted upon us by our patient's unwitting identification with his symbiotic (m)other.

Over time, through countertransference responsiveness, the confrontation slowly forms in our minds and bodies: "This has got to stop, I refuse to take any more of this misunderstanding and maltreatment. You are not relating to *me*! Subtext: "I'm only hired help and I have shown you that I can do it your way, the way you learned relatedness in early childhood. But as Exhibit A of other kinds of relationships in the world, you can't be this way and get away with it. You've got to stop this crappy way of engaging people and pay attention to who each important person in your life really is! The buck stops here!"

Now, of course, we never say any of this directly because the countertransference frustration is always heavily imbued with our own ways of experiencing exasperating interpersonal situations. But we do have to trust our feelings, our sense of our own being, our sense of our own individuated selves. *Our confrontation is not us confronting our clients, or even us confronting their behavior—our confrontation must be carefully aimed at the emotional template or symbiotic scenario that each client brings to the interpersonal field.*

And so we struggle to survive in the morass we are being handed. We struggle to formulate what's going on. We consult with colleagues trying to sort out countertransference in the narrow, personal sense from countertransference that might be usable in the broader interpersonal field to enhance mutual relatedness. We know we have been snared in our own enactments, but we aren't exactly sure just how this is happening—understanding will require an intersubjective engagement which, as the professional in the room, we must begin.

We sense the moment to strike is coming—the moment to confront what's happening between us, the moment to "stand against" the scenario being haplessly foisted upon us, the moment to stand up for ourselves in all this fray!

Don, you tell us with hindsight that for several weeks before this session you had somehow sensed something big coming, through you were not quite sure what or how. Also, with hindsight you can see that William entered this hour with some fresh openness which you must have unconsciously perceived—you begin the hour with, "One day William arrived for his session in a state of extreme upset." Neither you nor William was consciously aware of the nature of the upset or of the openness to new experience you both sensed was present—you from your curiosity and he from his extreme upset. Something huge was about to happen and you both sensed it.

So William launches into the upsetting spat he had had with his wife the evening before. In adversarial mode, you lie in wait watching the minutes tick by, waiting for your opportunity to take advantage of what you unconsciously perceive as a new vulnerability. You run down your countertransference checklist to be sure that whatever you are about to do truly feels likes it's for William and not just for you. Your sword is drawn and, with time quickly running out, you quickly strike! "Maybe you should have called me." Tears, relief, gratitude. William is run-through, pierced to the heart with love. "Maybe you should have called me."

In the aftermath of the moment, it occurs to you that in all the years of hospitals and recovery from his horrible life-threatening automobile accident in college William never once called out for a witness, for someone to recognize his pain, discouragement, and fear, for someone to be emotionally dependent and vulnerable with, for a *Partner in Thought*. Life-shattering sobs ensue—the spell of the symbiosis has been broken.

In the role-reversal countertransference we could say that you spoke what William as a child could never speak to his parents. "Mother, in all of your narcissistic loneliness *you should have called me*—called on me to be your beautiful baby whom you could grow through by nurturing, reflecting, and witnessing my developing being." "Father, you could have escaped you self-imposed isolation and frail sense of manliness if you had just called on me your beautiful, God-given son, to reflect your own proud fathering. But you did not call. Instead, you taught me not to be vulnerable, not to know my own dependency, not to call out for help in growing."

And then follows the *piece de resistance* of the hour, the precipitating morning event with his wife and children turning their backs on their walk to school and leaving William painfully behind—the event that triggered William's opening extreme upset and signaled to you a new openness was available and at last an opportunity for you to "stand against" his lifelong scenario of emotional isolation and pain.

Simultaneous with William's emotional break-through, you let us know, that your part of the mutual enactment broke. Your confrontation of William's scenario that you had been hooked into for so long—"Maybe you should have called me"—came from a deep sense of *me, myself, and I*, from a deep sense of *what's right for me if I'm allowed to be a real person in this relationship. In one passionate adversarial moment two people experienced a new degree of relational freedom. "Maybe you should have called me."*

Stern, in response to my comments said, "Relational Listening Perspectives are very useful to have in mind because they draw your attention as a clinician to the various ways you can always hear the material. Sometimes we follow our own paths and forget about the others, and Listening Perspectives offers a reminder that there are always those four ways of making sense and relational impact."

Summary: Developmental-Relational Listening to the Symbiosis

This Listening Perspective approach to what have been called Borderline and Characterological Personality Organizations is the product of many writers and researchers and stands firmly based on a long tradition of Ego and Self Psychology followed by later influences from the Interpersonalist and Relational traditions. Listening to symbiotic issues focuses on the experience of self which is fused or merged imperceptibly with the other—the "merger other." Kernberg (1975) holds that borderlines present "stable ego pathology" with "primitive defenses" which require "a modified psychoanalytic technique." Giovacchini (1979b) speaks of the "helpless patient" while others speak of the "difficult patient" or even the "obnoxious patient." Volkan (1976) and Kernberg (1976) urge a consideration of "primitive object relations." Mahler (1975) points to the developmental phenomena surrounding the early mother-child "symbiosis." Searles (1969) suggests that studies of "countertransference" yield critical information while Spotnitz (1976) highlights "underdeveloped aggression" as a central concept. Masterson (1972, 1976) presents the idea of an "abandonment depression" as the universal experience of borderlines in response to inadequate mothering. Stolorow and Lachman (1980) focus on "prestages of defense" and "developmental arrests." Stone (1980) has proposed a "three dimensional cube approach" based on a study of "constitutional, personality and adaptational factors." Balint (1968) points to the early area of personality development he calls "the basic fault." Margaret Little (1981) speaks of "basic unity" and "primary total undifferentiatedness." Kohut (1971) has isolated one group of preoedipal conditions as "narcissistic disorders" but still considers borderline phenomena essentially psychotic in nature.

The complexities encountered in understanding borderline states have necessitated new conceptual approaches primarily due to the general observation that borderline states are not reliably available to verbal-interpretive transference analysis nor do they improve significantly through a traditional analytic study of conflict, defense and resistance. Psychodynamic developmental psychology as applied to the study of borderline conditions focuses on the experience of a merger other and on defining (1) what functions and integrations have or have not developed, (2) the conditions under which they are and are not available, and (3) the relationships of the developed and undeveloped functions to each other and to the external world. That is, the interest is in observing and defining various specific and non-specific limitations in development and in understanding the many convoluted and/or distorted coping or adjustment attempts which have appeared to obscure or compensate for atypical development in the pre-oedipal and precohesive self periods of psychological development. The psychological structures built during this era may be regarded as retained relatedness modes from the early mutual cueing processes, overlearned ways for two to interact.

While the split affects characteristic of this period tend to make one search for heaven and fear hell in relationships, the subtleties and peculiarities of each symbiotic dance are what interest us most in therapeutic study. The search to define one's symbiotic modes is always unique, for they are always highly idiosyncratic, strange, and usually shocking to our higher sensibilities because they originate in early development. One woman experienced great relief when she finally could say, with violent shaking and tears, "I am nothing." At a pre-birth level, she now believes she was not desired by either of her parents and that she was emotionally handed over to another family member before she was born. To her parents she was "nothing," Her instinctive or unconscious knowledge of this situation, perhaps even in utero, governed all subsequent "layerings" of self and other experience. Most of her childhood developed as a reaction formation of extreme determination to be something or somebody everywhere she went. Through good-enough parenting she became a well-developed woman, but every aspect of her relatedness potential bore the mark in one way or another of "I am nothing." At every juncture in analysis the "nothing" appeared as indeed something very important to define and analyze in its impact.

One man was finally able to state with conviction, "My deepest passion is to be beaten, raped, robbed, and left for dead." Another, "I have a hard dick for women who can't be there for me." Or another, "I wish to be passive until I am finally abandoned altogether." Or, "My deepest longing is for an empty teat." These statements of a person's scenario reflect years of psychoanalytic work and in each case are radically condensed into an almost bizarre bottom line that captures the deepest and worst of one's perverted relatedness desires and potentials based on some of the earliest relatedness strivings. This kind of deep realization about one's passionate involvements with others is usually reflected in unconscious sexual longings of a perverse, self-destructive, or masochistic destructive, nature. Unconscious masturbation or orgasm phantasies, as they come to light in analytic work, always strike one as perverse or self-destructive in one way or another but regularly point toward one's deepest relational strivings. Short-term or non-analytic therapies rarely produce narrations of such basic symbiotic structures.

Ingmar Bergman's films have been particularly adept at capturing the essences of these perverse characterological passions that originate in symbiotic interactions. It is as though an infant learns that the excitement or passion of being with mother results from relinquishing certain crucial aspects of his or her instinctual longings or true self. This painful surrender of aspects of self comes to punctuate regularly all of our relatedness strivings, especially in our intimate love relations. Adult sexuality in its many (polymorphous perverse) variations becomes witness to the early necessity of giving up selected aspects of self need or striving in order to have and to enjoy the excitement of being with the other. Thus all passionate attachments can be expected to bear the stultifying influence of our personal conditioning and histories.

Igmar Bergman's film, *The Passion of Anna*, graphically depicts the unfolding of Anna's compulsive desire to maim, kill, or sacrifice the object of her passion, thus leaving her lost and lonely. Bergman shows how that scenario interacts with Peter's reciprocal passion toward being crushed, crumpled, and distorted in love. Peter's definition of his long and tenaciously held deformed version of potency and his desire for undistorted phallic potency is depicted in the last scene in which he is caught against the horizon, pacing back and forth between the image of a bent, gnarled, deformed tree and a tall, straight, healthy tree. Peter is frozen between the two trees, between the self-destructive passion of the old and the prospects of escape to new forms of self potency as the final scene potency fades. As usual, Bergman has succeeded in capturing a universal human dilemma nowhere more evident than in our earliest patterns of relatedness spoken of in this book as organizing and symbiotic.

I have spoken against content-oriented therapies in favor of process-oriented therapies since the earliest glimmerings of personality are formed within a context of interpersonal relationships and can only become known as emotional relatedness becomes re-created in later intimate relationships. The therapist must be prepared to simply relate, to shoot from the hip, as it were. To simply use his or her best relational skills and then carefully note what transpires. Both participants will be caught in mutually enacting early relationship modes and in dissociating the earliest "not-me" parts of their personalities (Stern 2010).

Relational interventions then become a matter of perceiving what is happening and then mutually formulating it or realizing it (Stern, in press) in order for greater relational flexibility and freedom to result.

Part IV

Summary and Conclusions

The Realization of Relational Interventions

I promised you in the title of this book that I would offer some interventional ideas regarding how to treat—how to be with—people often referred to as "borderline, bipolar, psychotic, and character disordered." I hope that I have started you on a fresh path or have encouraged you along an already familiar path toward discovering the importance of relationally-oriented process interventions.

Clinical research in Southern California involving more than 300 therapists over a forty year period has demonstrated that clients formerly considered "difficult-to-treat" or "untreatable" can, in fact, be successfully engaged in long-term, intense relational psychotherapy (Hedges 1983, 1992, 1994a,b,c, 2000b, 2005, 2013,b,c).

We have found that neither the symptom picture *per se* nor the subjective concerns of either the client or therapist preclude major transformational work. Rather, what limits the work are (1) the treatment orientation of the therapeutic dyad and/or (2) the combined personal and financial resources of the dyad. We have found that significant changes in relational flexibility and freedom are the outcome of the combined efforts and resources of both participants in an intense ongoing intersubjective relational involvement. Effective psychotherapy work does, however, require considerable time and emotional intensity on the part of both therapist and client.

By "the treatment orientation of the therapeutic dyad" I refer to the relinquishment by both of our field's former medicalized approaches to psychotherapy and the adoption of an approach committed to mutual conscious-raising through ongoing relational processes and processing. By "the combined personal and financial resources of the dyad" I mean the capacity and willingness of both participants to devote the time and emotional energy required to establish a robust project of reciprocal relating over a significant period of time.

The psychological pictures we have been considering in this book develop in the earliest months and years of life as the result of some form of relational trauma not necessarily obvious to others at the time. Early relational fears necessarily influence how subsequent relationships and relational learning situations become experienced. Early-learned relational modes that limit personality development are understandably entrenched in personality and only yield to a long-term, intense process of affective relating that serves to release constrictions that limit a person's relational flexibility and freedom. Clearly I do not see this form of therapy as an easy undertaking. But it can be very rewarding. Experience demonstrates that along the way both participants usually require some form of auxiliary support—case consultation or supervision for the therapist and outside consultative and/or support group experience for the client.

When Heinz Kohut (1984, p. 8) presciently envisioned what therapy work with borderline and psychotic clients might eventually look like—i.e., the development of an independent cohesive self *de novo* in therapy as in earliest life—he understood that the emotional strain would be immense on the part of the therapist. In order to accomplish this the client would need to be able to lean heavily on the therapist's emotional resources and psychic structures for protracted periods of time. Kohut also grasped the unbearably frightening and painful experience that the client would necessarily have to endure in giving up identity structures that have protected her for a lifetime against prepsychological chaos while she simultaneously reaches toward new, uncertain-feeling interpersonal affect regulation modes offered by the therapist and the therapeutic relationship.

The Listening Perspectives Approach

The treatment orientation utilized in the Southern California clinical research project replaces the medical objectivist epistemology with a set of listening perspectives that utilize metaphors based on studies of relational development. These developmental metaphors describe an array of relatedness possibilities from the simplest possibilities that are thought to characterize early life to the more complex possibilities that develop with age and experience. Along this axis of relational complexity four relational listening perspectives have been defined along with seven relational fears thought to be characteristic of different levels of relatedness complexity. These listening perspectives are not aimed at describing stages of human development, rather they represent ways of considering from different vantage points what interactional processes may be occurring at any moment in time during the course of psychotherapy. While the perspectives may at first appear to be only ways of describing the client's relational experiences of the therapist, they also describe the therapist's relational experiences of the client as well as the relational matrix wherein each meets the other at the horizons of their experience.

The subject matter of this book—the so-called "borderline, bipolar, psychotic, and character disordered" features of personality—are best listened to in the first two developmental listening perspectives, those for organizing and symbiotic relational experiences.

In this set of relational metaphors, the first fear an infant encounters when reaching out to organize living channels to the interpersonal environment is the fear that there will be no recognizing responsiveness from the other resulting in the disappointing experience of being left alone so that she withers and slumps. The second fear is that in the course of reaching for recognizing otherness she will encounter relational pain rather than pleasure and so she physically and mentally constricts and withdraws.

It follows then that in therapy the first relational task when treating the organizing experience in whatever forms it may take, is to establish sufficient relational safety to permit either a revitalization of the withered connection or a relaxation of the body-mind-relationship constriction. Only by fostering connection first can the disengaging or disconnecting transference be fruitfully studied in the here-and-now of the therapeutic relationship.

In the second listening perspective symbiotic channels for affect regulation of various types have developed into a set of relational expectancies based on what the child can establish with her early caregivers. Margaret Mahler (1968) has called the *internalization* of these expectancies the experience of symbiosis or of intersubjective oneness with the other. When exchanges with the social environment conform to the emotional expectancies of the established internalized symbiotic scenarios there is a sense of pleasure and goodness. When the exchanges do not meet with the hoped for or expected symbiotic interactions there is a sense of pain or badness followed by distress and rage. The third relational fear is, then, the fear of emotional abandonment which leads to insecure attachments and is marked by the good-bad affect splitting (you're with me or against me). The fourth fear results when the growing child is showing signs of developing her own mind and of individuating from the mothering person by reaching out beyond the symbiotic orb when she is then met with negative consequences or crushing opposition so that she either learns to conform (false self) or harshly rebels.

It follows then that in therapy the relational task when treating the symbiosis—in whatever forms it may take—is to allow the sequences of relational expectations to enter the therapeutic relationship so that they can become known by two—for the scenarios to be replicated in the therapeutic relationship, as it were. This is trickier than it sounds because we are talking about "knee-jerk" relational activities from both sides of the therapeutic relationship interacting so that one or the other or both can have a "new perception" of what's going on (Stern 2010, in press). But once seen, the pattern of the symbiotic scenario must be relinquished on both sides in order for both to achieve more relational flexibility or freedom. Stern speaks of the movement toward the relinquishment event has having an adversarial quality while I speak of it being a relational confrontation.[4]

Distinguishing Between Organizing and Symbiotic Experiences

The four different listening perspectives are *metaphoric abstractions* designed to define specific ways of relating by the client and therapist in the therapeutic encounter. The beauty of metaphors is that they give us a concrete picture of something familiar that helps us understand something not so easy to grasp. The beauty of abstractions is that they reduce complexities into a streamlined manageable schema. But neither metaphors nor abstractions do justice to the ineffable qualities of our minds or how we interact with each other in the therapeutic relationship.

I have advocated prioritizing relational processes over therapeutic content in order to give us an important lever with which to elucidate transference and countertransference. But we still are stuck with a continuous cascade of contents, behaviors, and symptoms that need empathic attention. It is a daunting task to sort through the vast array of content in order to get a fix on the relational process involved and we often find ourselves sorting, then resorting, then when something new comes up sorting yet again trying to get at the essence of the relational activity involved.

As I stressed earlier, most of us live many relational possibilities in different ways throughout every day. People who have experienced less than optimal psychological development may live a much more restricted array of possibilities on a regular basis. So when a relational move is puzzling how do we place it in the array of developmental possibilities and does it really matter? I believe it very much matters how we hear something because that will determine our recognizing responsiveness. For example, I believe the most common error we make on a regular basis is to listen to content as though it comes from the verbal-symbolic level of relatedness (listening perspective IV) when in fact what is being said has a relational purpose very different and more concrete than the words would lead us to believe. We simply don't listen and respond to a six-month-old and a toddler, or a kindergarten child, or a teenager in the same way. We titrate our understanding and recognition to fit the developmental level of the subjective experience we are responding to.

What then would be the point of distinction between hearing something as likely stemming from an organizing or, in contrast, a symbiotic experience. The answer is *the intention*. Transference at the organizing level is in the service of disconnecting, of disengaging from relatedness because in similar earlier relatedness ventures one was left unresponded to or injured.

On the other hand, transference at the symbiotic level relates to whether we are conforming or failing to conform to the relatedness expectations of the internalized scenario. That is, in the earlier stages of therapy we simply foster engagement in whatever ways seem possible so we can discern a person's symbiotic scenarios—sequences of expectation, as it were. When we conform we are good and the relating goes on well. But when we fail to conform to expectations we are immediately experienced as bad, as abandoning the emotional relatedness scenario in place at the moment. That is, transference of the symbiotic experience is represented by the good and bad affects associated with relational activities. Transference acts in the service of maintaining relating, even if it may seem to an outsider as somewhat skewed relating. Said differently, the intention of organizing transference activities is to disrupt connections while the intention of the symbiotic transference is to connect or to maintain a connection with a certain kind of relatedness scenario.

So What Are Relational Interventions?

When we grasp that psychotherapy is basically about helping people with their relationships our task is greatly clarified. We aim to intervene in some way in people's habitual ways of relating. Relational habits are transferred from the past into the present and so we are looking to help people understand how their relational habits from past relationships are getting in the way in current relationships.

When Sigmund Freud began this therapeutic enterprise he only knew how to focus on transferences originating in the complex verbal-symbolic level of independent and triangular relating (listening perspective IV). It took Heinz Kohut until 1971 to be able to spell out transferences formed in the period of consolidation of self (listening perspective III). While many gifted clinicians have been studying the problem for many years, only now are we becoming fairly clear about the kinds of transference experience that date back to the symbiotic era (listening perspective II) and the organizing era (listening perspective I). In each listening perspective we have the challenge to understand what kinds of relating do we and our clients actually do? In each perspective we have the challenge to actually relate to the client in such a way that their relational habits or constrictions can become known and new relational freedoms can be experienced.

In the organizing level we intervene at the moments of disconnecting transference by encouraging—and perhaps at times even demanding—that they stay emotionally present rather than engage in some kind of disconnecting activity. Since we can't emotionally intervene in disconnections unless there are connections, we spend a good part of the early period of therapy establishing safe ways we can be together.

In the symbiotic level we intervene by standing against the scenario that they want us to participate in because it constricts our relational freedoms just as it constricts theirs. The early part of therapy is devoted to inviting any kind of relatedness that is personally and professionally tolerable so that we can learn what their relational habits are so they can be opposed in relational ways.

Appendix A

Informed Consent for Long-Term Psychotherapy Regarding a Case Monitor, Medical Care, and Termination Plans

[Also for Use When There is a History of Trauma]

Psychotherapy that lasts for more than twenty sessions or six months necessarily involves an ongoing relationship between you and your therapist. One of the purposes of long-term, intensive psychotherapy is to allow your past emotional patterns to emerge and to be understood as they affect current relationships, particularly the therapeutic relationship. If there is the possibility that early or deep trauma of any kind affected your development, then as a part of your therapy you may need to review or to reexperience the emotions that were attached to that trauma.

Experience with revived memories of early abuse, deprivation, and trauma tells us that these memories are usually confusing, frightening, and/or upsetting. Experience in psychotherapy further tells us that such early memories are not usually recorded only in ordinary recollections, pictures of the events, or stories, but *in the ways we experience relationships and in various muscles and tissues of our bodies*. Thus, when these memories emerge in the here and now to be looked at they will be manifest in the ways you experience your therapist and/or the ways you experience your body and mind in reaction to therapy or to the therapeutic relationship.

There are three main dangers of intensive, long-term, relational psychotherapy:

1. You may begin to experience your therapist as somehow frightening, dangerous, neglectful, or not "on your side" in some way in the therapy process.

2. You may experience body reactions that represent early memories—such as agitation, distress, apathy, addictions, depression, eating and sleeping difficulties, confusion, suspiciousness, or other physical symptoms intruding into your life in various ways.

3. You may feel a strong urge to flee, emotionally or physically, from your therapy so as to avoid further emergence of bad memories or negative experiences.

Psychotherapists have developed standard ways of addressing these three potential dangers:

1. There may come a time when your confidence in your therapist or in the therapeutic process begins to get shaky. It is important that you first bring this up with your therapist and then, if your concerns continue, to arrange with him or her to seek out a third-party professional case monitor or consultant with whom to discuss your misgivings. Your therapist will help you locate a mental health professional who is familiar with this kind of work and who can listen carefully to what problems are coming up with your therapist or with the therapy process and make appropriate suggestions and recommendations. If your therapist at any time believes your emotional reactions are threatening to

you or to your therapy in any way, he or she will insist that you immediately consult a mutually agreed-upon case monitor.

2. An increase in any physical symptoms or adverse emotional reactions during the course of long-term psychotherapy usually signals the emergence of early traumatic memories. For your well-being and safety, it may be essential for you to have immediate medical and/or psychiatric evaluation and to remain under the care of a physician for a period of time. If your therapist at any time feels that the physical or mental reactions emerging in the course of treatment may potentially endanger you in any way, he or she will insist that you go immediately for medical and/or psychiatric consultation.

3. Should you wish to terminate treatment before you and your therapist mutually agree upon a beneficial time, it may be that you are unconsciously wanting to avoid the emergence of long-hidden traumatic memories. For example, you may experience your therapist as somehow failing you, as repeating previous insults or abuse to you, or as not being interested in you, not being emotionally available, not understanding you, or not liking you. You may then abruptly want to stop seeing your therapist in order to avoid the emotional pain and/or perceived dangers of dealing with these issues. Your first remedy would likely be to consult a mutually agreed-upon case monitor (as specified in item 1, above) in order to discuss the issues coming up with your therapist or your therapy process. A part of this consultation will be that your therapist and case monitor will communicate with each other about the relevant issues. Additionally, it is of crucial importance that you be willing to continue at least five to ten therapy sessions so that you, your

therapist, and your case monitor can adequately discuss your reasons for wanting to stop therapy and try to reach a joint understanding of what these reasons may mean to you and to your ongoing therapy process. If your therapist feels your decision to terminate therapy is abrupt or may be related to the revival of early traumatic memories, he or she may, in your best interest, insist that you consult a case monitor and then continue for a series of five to ten additional sessions before terminating.

Informed Consent Agreement

I have read the above considerations for entering into long-term, in-depth relational psychotherapy. I understand that certain dangers may be expected to appear over time in relational therapy especially when there is a history of past trauma. I have discussed the dangers and the usual safeguards listed above with my therapist so that I understand them. If any of the above conditions occur—(1) the loss of confidence in the therapy or the therapist, (2) the emergence or increase of physical or mental symptoms, or (3) the wish to terminate before a mutually agreed-upon time—I agree to abide by the three safeguards listed above, that is (1) to consult with a third-party professional case monitor, (2) to consult with a medical/psychiatric practitioner, and/or (3) to attend five to ten regular termination sessions to discuss the impasse fully.

I further understand that this informed consent and other written requests that my therapist may make from time to time pertaining to my well-being and safety must be agreed upon in order to enter further into or to continue long-term psychotherapy. Failure to comply with any requirements that are designed to safeguard me and my therapy process will be grounds for my therapist to give me a five to ten sessions notice of termination. This agreement supplements previous informed consents.

_____

Client Signed   Date

_____

Therapist Signed   Date

Appendix B

Informed Consent Regarding Limited Physical Contact during Psychotherapy

I, _____,

hereby grant permission to my therapist to engage in limited and token forms of physical contact with me as a part of our ongoing psychotherapy process.

I understand that the purpose of therapeutic touching is to actualize for study, in concrete physical forms, certain basic aspects of human contact that I may have been deprived of or that may have been distorted in my personal development.

I understand that the purpose of therapeutic touching is not for gratification of physical longings, nor for providing physical comfort or support. Rather, the specific forms and times of the limited physical therapeutic contact are aimed toward understanding issues around the approach to, the achievement of, the sustaining of, and/or the breaking off of human emotional contact.

I understand that limited forms of physical contact such as handshakes, "A.A. type" hugs (Alcoholics Anonymous bear hugs), occasional hand holding, and other token physical gestures are not uncommon as a part of the interpersonal process of psychotherapy. However, other forms of touching are more rare and need to be clearly understood by both parties and discussed in terms of their possible meanings.

I understand that many professional psychotherapists believe that physical contact of any sort is inappropriate because it fails to encourage verbalization and symbolization of exactly what meanings might be implicit in the physical touch.

I understand that sexual touching of any type is unethical, illegal, and never a part of professional psychotherapy.

I understand that many aspects of the psychotherapeutic process, including the possible value of limited physical contact, cannot be fully established as clearly beneficial on a scientific basis. But I also understand that physical contact has many values in human relationships and that to categorically exclude it from the psychotherapeutic relationship may be detrimental to my therapeutic process when the critical focus for study needs to be around concrete and personal experiences of meaningful interpersonal contact.

I HEREBY AGREE THAT SHOULD I HAVE ANY MISGIVINGS, DOUBTS, OR NEGATIVE REACTIONS to therapeutic physical contact or to the anticipation of such, I will immediately discuss my concerns with my therapist.

If for any reason I experience concerns that I am reluctant to discuss directly with my therapist, or if I feel unsatisfied with our discussion, I HEREBY AGREE TO SEEK IMMEDIATE THIRD-PARTY PROFESSIONAL CONSULTATION FROM A LICENSED PSYCHOTHERAPIST MUTUALLY AGREED UPON BY MY THERAPIST AND MYSELF. This part of the agreement is to ensure that no misunderstandings or uncomfortable feelings arise as a result of physical contact or the anticipation of therapeutic physical touching.

I understand that I may at any time choose to discontinue this permission by a mutual exchange of written acknowledgments indicating that permission for therapeutic physical contact is revoked.

I HAVE CAREFULLY READ ALL OF THE ABOVE PROVISIONS AND HAVE DISCUSSED THEM WITH MY THERAPIST. ANY QUESTIONS OR MISGIVINGS I HAVE ARE WRITTEN IN THE SPACE PROVIDED BELOW. This agreement supplements previous informed consents.

SPECIFIC QUESTIONS, MISGIVINGS, AND CONCERNS:

_____
Client   Date

_____
Therapist   Date

ADDITIONAL REQUESTS:

_____
Request   Initial   Date

_____
Request   Initial   Date

Appendix C

A Brief History of Psychiatric Diagnoses

Although this book is about the psychotherapy relationship and not about psychiatric diagnosis or treatment, since diagnosis has been an important part of our professional history I want here to briefly touch on this history so that the main text could move forward without detractions.

"Borderline" has been used over time to mean many things. Originally, "borderline psychosis" awkwardly described a person who appeared normal/neurotic enough but who from time to time would lapse into psychotic episodes. A major breakthrough in diagnostic understanding occurred in Otto Kernberg's 1976 book, *Borderline Personality Organization* in which he defined borderline as *an essentially relational problem* that defied clear nosological definition. To speak of a way personality attributes are interpersonally organized is a giant step away from descriptive *DSM* formulations. According to Kernberg and the many clinicians and theoreticians who followed him, borderline persons were thought to develop and to retain in the organization of their personalities certain fixed ways of experiencing relationships that originated in their symbiotic phase of development—defined by Margaret Mahler (1968) as 4 to 24 months of age.

The ensuing *Psychodynamic Diagnostic Manual* (*PDM* 2006) defines *"borderline-level" relating* as between normal/neurotic and psychotic levels of relating. That is:

Higher = normal/neurotic relational issues

Borderline = character relational issues

Lower = psychotic/bipolar/schizophrenic relational issues

The *Psychodynamic Diagnostic Manual* is a collaborative effort of

- The American Psychoanalytic Association
- The International Psychoanalytical Association
- The Division of Psychoanalysis (39) of the American Psychological Association
- The American Academy of Psychoanalysis and Dynamic Psychiatry
- The National Membership Committee on Psychoanalysis in Clinical Social Work

The *PDM* is a diagnostic framework that attempts to characterize an individual's full range of functioning—the depth as well as the surface of emotional, cognitive, and social patterns. It emphasizes individual variations as well as commonalities. The *PDM* is based on current neuroscience, treatment outcome research, and other empirical investigations. Research on brain development and the maturation of mental processes suggests that patterns of emotional, social, and behavioral functioning involve many areas of personality working together rather than in isolation. The *PDM* notes that process-oriented research has demonstrated that essential characteristics of the psychotherapeutic relationship as conceptualized by psychodynamic models (i.e., the working alliance, transference phenomena, and stable characteristics of patient and therapist) are more predictive of outcome than any designated treatment approach *per se.* The *PDM* uses a multidimensional approach to describe the intricacies of the patient's overall functioning and ways of engaging in the therapeutic process.

The *PDM* (I) begins with a classification of the spectrum of personality patterns and disorders, then (II) offers a "profile of mental functioning" covering in more detail the patient's capacities, and finally (III) considers symptom patterns, with emphasis on the patient's subjective experience. Here is a thumbnail overview of this essentially relational approach which I will soon contrast with the cognitive-behavioral approach of the *DSM.*

DIMENSION I: PERSONALITY PATTERNS AND DISORDERS—P Axis

The *PDM* classification of personality patterns takes into account two areas: (1) the person's general location on a continuum from healthier to more disordered functioning, and (2) the nature of the characteristic ways the individual organizes mental functioning and engages the world.

DIMENSION II: MENTAL FUNCTIONING—M AXIS

The second *PDM* dimension offers a more detailed description of emotional functioning—the capacities that contribute to an individual's personality and overall level of psychological health or pathology. It takes a more microscopic look at mental life, systematizing such capacities as information processing and self-regulation; the forming and maintaining of relationships; experiencing, Organizing, and expressing different levels of affects or emotions; representing, differentiating, and integrating experience; using coping strategies and defenses; observing self and others; and forming internal standards.

DIMENSION III: MANIFEST SYMPTOMS AND SUBJECTIVE CONCERNS —S AXIS

Dimension III begins with the *DSM-V-TR* categories and goes on to describe the affective states, cognitive processes, somatic experiences, and relational patterns most often associated clinically with each one.

> "We approach symptom clusters as useful descriptors. Unless there is compelling evidence in a particular case for such an assumption, we do not regard them as highly demarcated biopsychosocial phenomena. *PDM* nosology is explicitly set within a dynamic framework that focuses on the full range and depth of human mental functioning" (p. 13). "Therefore, our intent, in the various dimensions that comprise our nosological array, is to ascribe meanings, as best we can discern and formulate them, to the observed and described phenomena; i.e., symptoms, behaviors, traits, affects, attitudes, thoughts, fantasies, and so on" (p. 9).

In considering Borderline Personality Organization the *PDM* states,

> "Clinicians...have emphasized the affect-and impulse-regulation problems of individuals with borderline personality organization. They comment on the extremity and rawness of their clients' emotions and also on their excessive use of defenses that some theorists and researchers...have labeled "primitive" or "immature"—that

is, defenses that are more distorting than those most frequently used by neurotic level people....The most commonly noted of such defenses are splitting and projective identification. Splitting is the tendency to see self and others in moralized, all-good and all-bad categories....Projective identification involves failing to recognize troubling aspects of one's own personality, but feeling absolutely certain that another person (e. g., the therapist) has those undesirable qualities and treating that person accordingly—eventually evoking from the other person the attitudes that have been projected with such conviction.

Other Borderline Defenses omnipotent control (treating another as an extension of oneself, with little recognition that the other person is a separate human being with independent needs, desires, and preferences), [i.e., boundary problems] primitive idealization (seeing another as all good and larger than life as a small child might see an admired adult) and primitive devaluation (seeing another as completely worthless, with no redeeming qualities whatever)" (p. 93).

Acknowledging the pivotal role that countertransference has come to play in all borderline level character orientations the *PDM* states, "In contrast to the benign 'physicianly' attitude that patients with neurotic-level personality disorders tend to elicit in therapists and interviewers, patients at the borderline [level] evoke strong feelings that clinicians may have to struggle to manage or contain. Often these are negative feelings, such as hostility, fear, confusion, helplessness, or boredom, however, powerful rescue fantasies and wishes to cure the patient by love are also common" (p. 93).

Since the experience of character or borderline-level or relational symbiosis is developmentally universal, I will speak of a mental relational position that we all know from our own experience—a position midway between culturally validated sanity and idiosyncratic personal frames of mind that lack cultural consensus or endorsement and are generally considered crazy.

Borderline frames of mind can seem eminently sensible yet lack relational flexibility. Borderline frames of mind can seem quite convincing but they may lack interpersonal richness and fluidity. Often they are modulated by a "false self". We are often comfortable with borderline or symbiotic frames of mind in others because they match certain frames of mind that we ourselves have grown up with. That is, certain frames of mind resonate with us at a limbic system level (Lewis, et. al. 2000). Likewise, whatever our own symbiotic/borderline frames of mind may look like, whatever our internalized symbiotic scenarios may demand, we can become intensely uncomfortable with someone whose fundamental assumptions about relationships and symbiotic scenarios differ sharply from our own.

I have often said to students that if we were to write three pages of how people and relationships "should" and "should not" be, we would see laid out before us our own borderline scenarios. That is, a set of templates for proper and improper relatedness that seem straightforward enough to us would emerge. Of course, no two people would write the same things and many assumptions among us might be hotly debated. Where in our development do these highly idiosyncratic relational templates come from? Relational templates

146

arise from the early emotional attunement or attachment bond or symbiosis that develops from the mutual cuing and mutual affect regulation between infant and caregiver. Symbiotic relational templates organize and regulate stimulation arising from within the child as well as stimulation originating in the interpersonal world outside the child. All of the characterological pictures in diagnostic manuals have their origin in modes of relatedness that emotionally characterized the relational scenarios established in the symbiotic tie, so in that sense "character disorders" are mid-range between neurosis and psychosis and therefore borderline-level also.

In sharp contrast to mid-range borderline and character orientations, in what have been called "thought disorders" (i.e., the schizophrenias and other psychotic states) the symbiosis has not been able to contain and organize stimulation coming from outside the body in ways that conform to ordinary human cause and effect conventions so that the thoughts and behaviors seem strange, unconventional, or bizarre. On the other hand, when the symbiosis has been unsuccessful in Organizing and regulating the strong affective stimulation arising from within the body into an acceptable cultural bandwidth of affective experience and expression (high and low), we have what has been called an "affective disorder" (or a mood or bipolar disorder) that may range from chronically depressed to chronically manic, to cyclic, or episodic.

Because of the widespread influence of *The Diagnostic and Statistical Manual of the American Psychiatric Association* I want to here summarize the diagnostic criteria for "301.83 Borderline Personality Disorder" so we can see how far it strays from Kernberg's original intentions and the psychodynamic orientation of the *PDM*.

"General Description: A pervasive pattern of instability of interpersonal relationships, sell-image, and affects and marked impulsively beginning by early adulthood and present in a variety of contexts, as indicated by five (or more) of the following:

(1) frantic efforts to avoid real or imagined abandonment.
(2) a pattern of unstable and intense interpersonal relationships characterized by alternating between extremes of idealization and devaluation.
(3) identity disturbance: markedly and persistently unstable self-image or sense of self.
(4) impulsivity in at least two areas that are potentially self-damaging (e.g., spending, sex, substance abuse, reckless driving, binge eating)....
(5) recurrent suicidal behavior, gestures, or threats, or self-mutilating behavior.
(6) affective instability due to a marked reactivity of mood (e.g., intense episodic dysphoria, irritability, or anxiety usually lasting a few hours and only rarely more than a few days)....
(7) chronic feelings of emptiness.
(8) inappropriate, intense anger or difficulty controlling anger (e.g., frequent displays of temper, constant anger, recurrent physical fights).
(9) transient, stress-related paranoid ideation or severe dissociative symptoms" (pp. 325-326).

In summary, personality organization that features unconventional thoughts and behavior falls in the range often referred to as schizophrenic or psychotic. Ways of Organizing personality functioning that fall outside the cultural norm for affect experience and expression have been called affect, mood or bipolar disorders. Midway between culturally defined normal/neurotic personality organization and psychotic personality organization is borderline personality organization. The various character orientations or disorders fall within the mid- or borderline range in that they fail to meet cultural expectations of normality but also usually do not quality as psychotic.

Appendix D

Relational Listening I: Development, Transference, Countertransference

Age	Developmental Thrust	Transference	Countertransference
>3yrs	Self and Other Relational Experiences	From Independent, Ambivalently Held Others	Overstimulating Experiences as Distracting or Impediment
24 to 36 Months	Self-consolidating, Recognition Experiences	From Resonating or Injuring Self-Others	Facilitating Experiences of Fatigue, Boredom, and Drowsiness
4 to 24 Months	Symbiotic and Separating Scenarios/ Interactive Experience	From Interacting and Enacting Others– Replication	Resistive Experiences to Replicating Demanding, Dependent Scenarios
± 4 Months	Organizing Merger and Rupturing Experiences	From Engaging and Disengaging Others	Dread and Terror of Unintegrated Experiences

Relational Listening II:
Resistance, Listening Mode,
Therapeutic Intervention

Age	Resistance	Listening Mode	Therapeutic Intervention
>3yrs	To the Return of The Repressed	Evenly Hovering Attention Free Association Equidistance	Interpretive Reflection: Verbal-Symbolic Interpretation
24 to 36 Months	To Experiencing Narcissistic Shame and Narcissistic Rage	Resonance with Self-Affirmation, Confirmation, and Inspiration	Empathic Attunement to Self to Self-Other Resonance
4 to 24 Months	To Assuming Responsibility for Differentiating	Replicating and Renouncing Symbiotic and Separating Scenarios	Replication Standing Against the Symbiotic & Separating Scenarios: Reverberation
± 4 Months	To Bonding Connections and Engagements	Engagement: Connection, Interception, Linking	Focus On and Interception of Disengagements

Notes

[1] All forms of physical contact have been avoided in traditional psychoanalytic psychotherapy. However, it becomes clear that when the Organizing rupture in contact is being actively lived out, the client is in an extremely concrete state of mind, and adequate empathic contact may involve token "interpretive touching" in the specific manner just suggested. Elsewhere, I consider the many and complex issues involved in this concretized form of interpretation (Hedges, 1994a, c). Kohut's deathbed legacy involves just such interpretive touching. (p. 474)

[2] In the extended version of this case report (Hedges, 2000) I am able to show Paul how he is in fact doing what he is talking about to me during the process of this hour and how my tendency has been to comply with his constant severing of connection between us.

[3] I follow Mahler's intended use of the term symbiosis as a set of internalized interaction patterns that the infant develops in relation to early caregivers. Symbiosis as a term was borrowed by her from biology but she does not use it in a biological or sociological sense, rather in an internalized psychological sense. Margaret Little refers to this as "basic unity."

[4] There are two important bodies of work that parallel these formulations. One is the "recognition theory" of Jessica Benjamin in which, borrowing on the neuropsychological work of Alan Schore and Stephen Porges as well as the infant research of Daniel Stern and the Boston Process Change Group, she shows how at each moment in human developmental progression is marked by an emotional extension that is recognized (or not) by another so that the child and later the adult

can come to know herself (Benjamin 2013). Having one's extensions not recognized and responded to or responded to in a painful manner leads to the unfortunate withering and constricting responses in the organizing experience and to the formation of sequences of good and bad expectations in the symbiotic experience.

The other parallel body of work concerns dissociation theory and is led by Donnel Stern and Philip Bromberg writing in the Interpersonal/Relational psychotherapy tradition. Following Harry Stack Sullivan, they speak of parts of ourselves or "self-states" as coming to have a "good-me", a "bad-me" and a "not-me" aspect. We are generally aware of and live from the good-me part of ourselves while we do our best to ignore or set aside the bad-me parts. Dissociation theory focuses on various "not-me" parts that have been split off or isolated from consciousness and that get enacted in the therapeutic relationship by both client and therapist—until one of these adversarial moments when not-me parts are forced into recognition by one or the other of the dyad. Dissociated aspects of self in the organizing experience can be employed in either the engagement or disengagement processes. Dissociated aspects of self in the symbiotic experience become embedded in the expectations of one's scenarios.

References

Abraham. K. (1924). *Selected Papers on Psychoanalysis*. New York: International Universities Press.

Balint, A. (1943). On Identification. *International Journal of Psycho-Analysis* 24:97-107.

Balint, M. (1968). *The Basic Fault*. London: Tavistock Publications.

Beck, A.T., Dozois, D.J.A. (2011). Cognitive therapy: Current status and future directions. *Annual Review of Medicine*, 62: 397-409.

Blanck, G. and Blanck R. (1979). *Ego Psychology II: Psychoanalytic Developmental Psychology*. New York: Columbia University Press.

Bollas, C. (1987). *The Shadow of the Object: Psychoanalysis the Unthought Known*. New York: Columbia University Press.

Bromberg, P. (2011) *The Shadow of the Tsunami*. NY: Routledge.

Cozolino, L. (2002). *The Neuroscience of Psychotherapy: Building and Rebuilding the Human Brain (Norton Series on Interpersonal Neurobiology)*. New York: W.W. Norton.

_____(2006). *The Neuroscience of Human Relationships: Attachment and the Developing Social Brain.* New York: W.W. Norton

_____(2012).*The Social Neuroscience of Education*: Optimizing Attachment and Learning in the Classroom. New York: Norton.

Davies, J. M. (1994). Love in the Afternoon: A Relational Reconsideration of Desire and Dread in the Countertransference. *Psychoanalytic Dialogues*: 4:153-170.

Erikson, E. (1959). Identity and the Life Cycle. *Psychological Issues.* Monograph No. 1. New York: International Universities Press.

Fonagy, P., Gergely, G., Jurist, E. and Target, M. (2002). *Affect Regulation, Mentalization, and the Development of the Self.* New York: Other Press.

Fraiberg, S. (1982). Pathological defenses in infancy. *Psychoanalytic Quarterly,* 51:612-635.

Freud, A. (1936). *The Ego and the Mechanisms of Defense.* New York: International Universities Press.

Freud, S. (1912a). Papers on Technique. The Dynamics of Transference. *Standard Edition of The Complete Psychological Works of Sigmund Freud* 12:97-108.

_____(1912b). Papers on Technique. Recommendations to Physicians Practicing Psychoanalysis. *Standard Edition of The Complete Psychological Works of Sigmund Freud* 12:109-120.

_____(1915). Observations on Transference Love. *Standard Edition of The Complete Psychological Works of Sigmund Freud* 12:159-171.

_____(1923). The ego and the id. *Standard Edition of The Complete Psychological Works of Sigmund Freud* 19:3-68.

_____(1924). The Dissolution of the Oedipus Complex *Standard Edition of The Complete Psychological Works of Sigmund Freud* 19:172-179.

_____(1933). New introductory lectures on psycho-analysis. *Standard Edition of The Complete Psychological Works of Sigmund Freud* 22:1-184.

Giovacchini (1979b) *Treatment of Primitive Mental States.* New York: Jason Aronson.

Hedges, L. E. (1983). *Listening Perspectives in Psychotherapy.* Northvale, NJ: Jason Aronson Publishers [Twentieth Anniversary Edition, 2003].

_____(1992). *Interpreting the Countertransference.* Northvale, NJ: Jason Aronson Publishers.

_____(1994a). *In Search of the Lost Mother of Infancy.* Northvale, NJ: Jason Aronson Publishers.

_____(1994b). *Remembering, Repeating, and Working Through Childhood Trauma: The Psychodynamics of Recovered Memories, Multiple Personality, Ritual Abuse, Incest, Molest, and Abduction.* Northvale, NJ: Jason Aronson Publishers.

_____(1994c). *Working the Organizing experience: Transforming Psychotic, Schizoid, and Autistic States.* Northvale, NJ: Jason Aronson Publishers.

_____(1996). *Strategic Emotional Involvement: Using Countertransference Experience in Psychotherapy.* Northvale, NJ: Jason Aronson Publishers.

_____(2000a, 2007). *Facing the Challenge of Liability in Psychotherapy: Practicing Defensively.* Northvale, NJ: Jason Aronson.

_____(2000a). *Terrifying Transferences: Aftershocks of Childhood Trauma.* Northvale, NJ: Jason Aronson Publishers.

_____(2005). Listening Perspectives for Emotional Relatedness Memories. *Psychoanalytic Inquiry,* 25:4, 455-483.

_____(1997). Hedges, L., Hilton, R., Hilton, V., Caudill, B. *Therapists At Risk: Perils of the Intimacy of the Therapeutic Relationship.* Northvale, NJ: Jason Aronson Publishers

_____(2011). *Sex in Psychotherapy; Sexuality, Passion, Love, and Desire in the Therapeutic Encounter.* New York: Routledge.

_____(2012a). *Overcoming Relationship Fears.* International Psychotherapy Institution e-Book.

_____(2012b). *Cross-Cultural Encounters.* International Psychotherapy Institution e-Book.

_____(2012c). *Making Love Last.* International Psychotherapy Institution e-Book.

_____(2013a). *Overcoming Relationship Fears Workbook.* International Psychotherapy Institution e-Book.

_____(2013b). *The Relationship in Psychotherapy and Supervision.* International Psychotherapy Institution e-Book.

Hendrix, H. (1988). *Getting the Love You Want: A Guide for Couples.* New York: Harper Perennial.

Jacobson, E. (1954). The Self and Object World: Vicissitudes of Their Infantile Cathexis and Their Influence on Ideational and Affective Development. *The Psychoanalytic Study of the Child.* 9:75-127. New York: International Press.

_____(1964). *The Self and Object World.* New York: International Press

Kernberg O. F.(1975). *Borderline Personality Organization.* New York: Jason Aronson.

_____(1976). *Object-Relations Theory and Clinical Psychoanalysis.* New York Jason Aronson.

_____(1980). *Internal World and External Reality.* New York: Jason Aronson.

Klein, Melanie (1952). *Developments in Psycho-Analysis.* London: Hogarth Press.

Kohut, H. (1971). *The Analysis of the Self.* New York: International Universities Press

_____(1984). *How does Analysis Cure.* Chicago: University of Chicago Press.

Lewis, T., Amini, F., and Lannon, R. (2000). *A General Theory of Love.* New York: Random House.

Little, Margaret (1981). *Transference Neurosis: Transference Psychosis.* New York: Jason Aronson.

Lowen, A. (1971). *The Language of the Body.* New York: Collier Books.

Mahler, M. (1968). *On Human Symbiosis and the Vicissitudes of Individuation,* Vol. 1, *Infantile Psychosis.* New York: International Universities Press.

Masterson, James F. (1972). *Treatment of the Borderline Adolescent: A Developmental Approach.* New York: John Wiley and Sons.

_____(1976). *Psychotherapy of the Borderline Adult: A Developmental Approach.* New York: Brunner/Mazel Publishers.

Mitchell, S. (1988). *Relational Concepts in Psychoanalysis.* Cambridge, MA: Harvard University Press.

_____(1993). *Hope and Dread in Psychoanalysis.* New York: Basic Books.

_____(1997). *Influence and Autonomy in Psychoanalysis.* Hillsdale, NJ: The Analytic Press.

Norcross. J. (2002). *Psychotherapy Relationships that Work: Therapist Contributions and Responsiveness to Patients.* New York: Oxford.

PDM Task Force. (2006). *Psychodynamic Diagnostic Manual.* Silver Spring, MD: Alliance of Psychoanalytic Organizations

Schore, A. N. (2003). *Affect Regulation and Disorders of the Self.* New York: W. W. Norton & Company.

_____(2013). *The Science of the Art of Psychotherapy (Norton Series on Interpersonal Neurobiology).* New York: W. W. Norton & Company.

Searles (1965). *Collected Papers on Schizophrenia and Related Subjects.* New York: International Universities Press.

_____(1979). *Countertransference and Related Subjects. Selected Papers.* New York: International Universities Press.

Seaton-Bacon, A. (2000). I am going to die. In Hedges 2000b

Spotnitz, Human (1976). *Psychotherapy of Preoedipal Conditions: Schizophrenia and Severe Character Disorders.* New York: Jason Aronson.

Stern. D. B. (2010) *Partners in Thought: Working with Unformulated Experience, Dissociation, and Enactment.* New York: Routledge.

_____(In Press). *Relational Freedom: Working in the Interpersonal Field.* New York: Routledge.

Stolorow, R., and Atwood, G. (1992). *Contexts of Being: The Intersubjective Foundations of Psychological Life.* Hillsdale, NJ: Analytic Press.

Stolorow, R., Atwood, G., and Brandchaft, B. (1994). *The Intersubjective Perspective.* Northvale, NJ: Jason Aronson.

Turner-Miller, S. 'Night, Mother, In Hedges 1996.

Volkan, Vamik D. (1976). *Primitive Object Relations: A Clinical Study of Schizophrenia, Borderline and Narcissistic Patients.* New York: International Universities Press.

Young-Bruehl, E. and Dunbar, C. (2009). *One Hundred Years of Psychoanalysis: A Timeline: 1900-2000.* Toronto, Canada: Caversham Productions

Acknowledgements

More than three hundred therapists at the Newport Psychoanalytic Institute and the Listening Perspectives Study Center have actively contributed to the formation of this book over a forty-year period, most of whom have been named in my previous seventeen published books. Special recognition is due to Audrey Seaton-Bacon and Sally Turner-Miller for their courageous work reported in the present book. Throughout this time my daughter, Breta Hedges, has been a constant support as have been my other family members, Marcie, Jaden, Ray, and Daniel. My office manager, Monica Mello is to be thanked for the careful preparation of the manuscript. Thanks to Doug Citro who knows my work thoroughly and who carefully read and critiqued the draft of this book.

From the moment I sent my first book, *Listening Perspectives in Psychotherapy,* to Jason Aronson in 1982 and he sent back a contract by return mail he has been an enthusiastic supporter and contributor to all of my books. He instantly saw my project of creating listening perspectives and the epistemological implications for my relational approach to listening. In his retirement he has taken on the volunteer project of electronically publishing worthy psychotherapy books as free downloads. His contribution to our field has been immense over the years and we all owe him a debt of gratitude.

I am also pleased to credit the woman who has painstakingly edited all six of my electronic books on freepsychotherapybooks.org, Melonie Bell. Her efforts have been tireless and kept me enthusiastic about this project. The next one will be on trauma.

When Dr. Aronson first proposed that I try out the publication facilities of the International Psychotherapy Institute I had a hard time imagining publishing without royalties and without cost to readers. But this is a new global age of free internet sharing and I'm glad to be a part of it. The distribution already is utterly astounding—thousands of books are now in circulation in 192 countries! I hope you enjoy this book and check out my others as well as my website ListeningPerspectives.com and my online articles and video streaming continuing education courses for mental health professionals at sfrankelgroup.com. Send me your reactions: lhedges7@gmail.com .

I wish to express special gratitude to colleagues who have worked with me and offered suggestions as this summary statement of ideas developed over a thirty-year period has shaped up:

Anderson, Terry	Ammon, Barbara
Alvarez-Gray, Nan	Besteman, Judith
Bush, Paula	Cahgan, Laura
Carter, John	Citro, Doug
Cohn-Weiss, Sandra	Colvin, Jeannie
Colvin, Tim	Cox, Shirley
Davidson, Jolyn	Davidtz, Jennifer
Davison, Robert	Diskin, Sheila
Eimers, Antoinette	Goldman, Ann

Greenslade, Cindy

Harris, Steve

Law-Glassman, Mina

Lichman, Jeanne

Mayer, Krysclie

Mills, Cherie

Raskin, Ruth

Schwieger, Jeff

Sutherland, Phil

Trubenbach, Ted

Van Sweden, Robert

Woodward, Michele

Hafner, Quinn

Haynes, Laura

Lenhart, Deborah

Lucas, Laurie

Middler, Marcy

Morrill, Cathy

Rodiger, Georgiana

Smith, Barbara

Tobin. James

Turner-Miller, Sarah

Whitcomb, Robert

About the Author

Lawrence Hedges, Ph.D., Psy.D., ABPP, began seeing patients in 1966 and completed his training in child psycho-analysis in 1973. Since that time his primary occupation has been training and supervising psychotherapists, individually and in groups, on their most difficult cases at the Listening Perspectives Study Center in Orange, California. Dr. Hedges was the Founding Director of the Newport Psychoanalytic Institute in 1983 where he continues to serve as supervising and training analyst. Throughout his career, Dr. Hedges has provided continuing education courses for psycho-therapists throughout the United States and abroad. He has consulted or served as expert witness on more than 400 complaints against psychotherapists in 20 states and has published 21 books on various topics of interest to psychoanalysts and psychoanalytic psychotherapists, three of which have received the Gradiva Award for the best psychoanalytic book of the year. During the 2009 centennial celebration of the International Psychoanalytic Association, his 1992 book, *Interpreting the Countertransference*, was named one of the key contributions in the relational track during the first century of psychoanalysis. In 2015 Dr. Hedges was distinguished by being awarded honorary membership in the American Psychoanalytic Association for his many contributions to psychoanalysis.

Photograph courtesy Marcie Bell

Other Books Authored and Edited by Lawrence Hedges

Listening Perspectives in Psychotherapy (1983, Revised Edition 2003)

In a fresh and innovative format Hedges organizes an exhaustive overview of contemporary psychoanalytic and object relations theory and clinical practice. "In studying the Listening Perspectives of therapists, the author has identified himself with the idea that one must sometimes change the Listening Perspective and also the interpreting, responding perspective." –Rudolf Ekstein, Ph.D. Contributing therapists: Mary Cook, Susan Courtney, Charles Coverdale, Arlene Dorius, David Garland, Charles Margach, Jenna Riley, and Mary E. Walker. Now available in a Twentieth Anniversary edition, the book has become a classic in the field.

Interpreting the Countertransference (1992)

Hedges boldly studies countertransference as a critical tool for therapeutic understanding. "Hedges clearly and beautifully delineates the components and forms of countertransference and explicates the technique of carefully proffered countertransference informed interventions… [He takes the view] that all countertransferences, no matter how much they belong to the analyst, are unconsciously evoked by the patient." –James Grotstein, M.D. Contributing therapists: Anthony Brailow, Karen K. Redding, and Howard Rogers. Selected as one of the notable contributions to psychoanalysis during its first century—Elisabeth Young-Bruehl and Christine Dunbar (2009).

In Search of the Lost Mother of Infancy (1994)

"Organizing transferences" in psychotherapy constitute a living memory of a person's earliest relatedness experiences and failures. Infant research and psychotherapeutic studies from the past two decades now make it possible to define for therapeutic analysis the manifestations of early contact traumas. A history and summary of the Listening Perspective approach to psychotherapy introduces the book. Contributing therapists: Bill Cone, Cecile Dillon, Francie Marais, Sandra Russell, Sabrina Salayz, Jacki Singer, Sean Stewart, Ruth Wimsatt, and Marina Young.

Working the Organizing Experience: Transforming Psychotic, Schizoid, and Autistic States (1994)

Hedges defines in a clear and impelling manner the most fundamental and treacherous transference phenomena, the emotional experiences retained from the first few months of life. Hedges describes the infant's attempts to reach out and form organizing connections to the interpersonal environment and how those attempts may have been ignored, thwarted, and/or rejected. He demonstrates how people live out these primitive transferences in everyday significant relationships and in the psychotherapy relationship. A critical history of psychotherapy with primitive transferences is contributed by James Grotstein and a case study is contributed by Frances Tustin.

Remembering, Repeating, and Working Through Childhood Trauma: The Psychodynamics of Recovered Memories, Multiple Personality, Ritual Abuse, Incest, Molest, and Abduction (1994)

Infantile focal as well as strain trauma leave deep psychological scars that show up as symptoms and memories later in life. In psychotherapy people seek to process early experiences that lack ordinary pictoral and narrational representations through a variety of forms of transference and dissociative remembering such as multiple personality, dual relating, archetypal adventures, and false accusations against therapists or other emotionally significant people. "Lawrence Hedges makes a powerful and compelling argument for why traumatic memories recovered during psychotherapy need to be taken seriously. He shows us how and why these memories must be dealt with in thoughtful and responsible ways and not simply uncritically believed and used as tools for destruction." –Elizabeth F. Loftus, Ph.D. Nominated for Gradiva Best Book of the Year Award.

Strategic Emotional Involvement: Using the Countertransference in Psychotherapy (1996)

Following an overview of contemporary approaches to studying countertransference responsiveness, therapists tell moving stories of how their work came to involve them deeply, emotionally, and not always safely with clients. These comprehensive, intense, and honest reports are the first of their kind ever to be collected and published. Contributing therapists: Anthony Brailow, Suzanne Buchanan, Charles Coverdale, Carolyn Crawford, Jolyn Davidson, Jacqueline Gillespie, Ronald Hirz, Virginia Hunter, Gayle Trenberth, and Sally Turner-Miller.

Therapists at Risk: Perils of the Intimacy of the Therapeutic Relationship (1997)

Lawrence E. Hedges, Robert Hilton, and Virginia Wink Hilton, long-time trainers of psychotherapists, join hands with attorney O. Brandt Caudill in this *tour de force* which explores the multitude of personal, ethical, and legal risks involved in achieving rewarding transformative connections in psychotherapy today. Relational intimacy is explored through such issues as touching, dualities in relationship, interfacing boundaries, sexuality, countertransference, recovered memories, primitive transferences, false accusations against therapists, and the critical importance of peer support and consultation. The authors clarify the many dynamic issues involved, suggest useful ways of managing the inherent dangers, and work to restore our confidence in and natural enjoyment of the psychotherapeutic process.

Facing the Challenge of Liability in Psychotherapy: Practicing Defensively (2000, Revised 2017)

In this litigious age, all psychotherapists must protect themselves against the possibility of legal action; malpractice insurance is insufficient and does not begin to address the complexity and the enormity of this critical problem. In this book, Lawrence E. Hedges urges clinicians to practice defensively and provides a course of action that equips them to do so. After working with over a hundred psycho-therapists and attorneys who have fought unwarranted legal and ethical complaints from clients, he has made the fruits of his work available to all therapists. In addition to identifying those patients prone to presenting legal problems, Dr. Hedges provides a series of consent forms (on the accompanying disk), a compelling rationale for using them, and a means of easily introducing them into clinical practice. This book is a wake-up call, a practical, clinically sound response to a frightening reality, and an absolute necessity for all therapists in practice today. Now available in a revised and updated edition. Gradiva Award Best Book of the Year.

Terrifying Transferences: Aftershocks of Childhood Trauma (2000)

There is a level of stark terror known to one degree or another by all human beings. It silently haunts our lives and occasionally surfaces in therapy. It is this deep-seated fear—often manifest in dreams or fantasies of dismemberment, mutilation, torture, abuse, insanity, rape, or death—that grips us with the terror of being lost forever in time and space or controlled by hostile forces stronger than ourselves. Whether the terror is felt by the client or by the therapist, it has a disorienting, fragmenting, crippling power. How we can look directly into the face of such terror, hold steady, and safely work it through is the subject of *Terrifying Transferences*. Contributing therapists: Linda Barnhurst, John Carter, Shirley Cox, Jolyn Davidson, Virginia Hunter, Michael Reyes, Audrey Seaton-Bacon, Sean Stewart, Gayle Trenberth, and Cynthia Wygal. Gradiva Award Best Book of the Year.

Sex in Psychotherapy: Sexuality, Passion, Love, and Desire in the Therapeutic Encounter (2010)

This book takes a psychodynamic approach to understanding recent technological and theoretical shifts in the field of psychotherapy. Hedges provides an expert overview and analysis of a wide variety of new perspectives on sex, sexuality, gender, and identity; new theories about sex's role in therapy; and new discoveries about the human brain and how it works. Therapists will value Hedges' unique insights into the role of sexuality in therapy, which are grounded in the author's studies of neurology, the history of sexuality, transference, resistance, and countertransference. Clinicians will also appreciate his provocative analyses of influential perspectives on sex, gender, and identity, and his lucid, concrete advice on the practice of therapeutic listening. This is an explosive work of tremendous imagination and scholarship. Hedges speaks the uncomfortable truth that psychotherapy today often reinforces the very paradigms that keep patients stuck in self-defeating, frustrating behavior. He sees sexuality as a vehicle for both therapists and patients to challenge what they think they know about the nature of self and intimacy. This book is a must-read for anyone interested in understanding 21st-century human beings—or in better understanding themselves and their sexuality.

Cross-Cultural Encounters: Bridging Worlds of Difference (2012)

This book is addressed to everyone who regularly encounters people from other cultural, ethnic, socioeconomic, linguistic, and ability groups. Its special focus, however, is aimed at counselors, therapists, and educators since their daily work so often involves highly personal cross-cultural interactive encounters. The running theme throughout the book is the importance of cultivating an attitude of tentative and curious humility and openness in the face of other cultural orientations. I owe a great debt to the many students, clients, and friends with diverse backgrounds who over the years have taught me how embedded I am in my own cultural biases. And who have helped me find ways of momentarily transcending those biases in order to bridge to an inspiring and illuminating intimate personal connection.

Overcoming Our Relationship Fears (2012)

We are all aware that chronic tension saps our energy and contributes to such modern maladies as high blood pressure and tension headaches, but few of us realize that this is caused by muscle constrictions that started as relationship fears in early childhood and live on in our minds and bodies. Overcoming Our Relationship Fears is a user-friendly roadmap for healing our relationships by dealing with our childhood fear reflexes. It is replete with relationship stories to illustrate each fear and how we individually express them. Dr. Hedges shows how to use our own built-in "Aliveness Monitor" to gauge our body's reaction to daily interactions and how they trigger our fears. Exercises in the book will help us release these life-threatening constrictions and reclaim our aliveness with ourselves and others.

Overcoming Our Relationship Fears: WORKBOOK (2013)

Developed to accompany Hedges' Overcoming Relationship Fears, this workbook contains a general introduction to the seven relationship fears that are a part of normal human development along with a series of exercises for individuals and couples who wish to learn to how to release their Body-Mind-Relationship fear reflexes. An Aliveness Journal is provided for charting the way these fears manifest in relationships and body maps to chart their location in each person's body.

The Relationship in Psychotherapy and Supervision (2013)

The sea-change in our understanding of neurobiology, infant research, and interpersonal/relational psychology over the past two decades makes clear that we are first and foremost a relational species. This finding has massive implications for the relational processes involved in teaching and supervising psychotherapy. Clinical theory and technique can be taught didactically. But relationship can only be learned through careful attention to the supervisory encounter itself. This advanced text surveys the psychodynamic and relational processes involved in psychotherapy and supervision.

Making Love Last: Creating and Maintaining Intimacy in Long-term Relationships (2013)

We have long known that physical and emotional intimacy diminish during the course of long-term relationships. This book deals with the questions, "Why romance fades over time?" And "What can we do about it?" Relational psychologists, neuropsychologists, and anthropologists have devoted the last two decades to the study of these questions with never before available research tools. It is now clear that we are genetically predisposed to search out intersubjective intimacy from birth but that cultural systems of child rearing seriously limit our possibilities for rewarding interpersonal relationships. Anthropological and neurological data suggests that over time we have been essentially a serially monogamous species with an extraordinary capacity for carving out new destinies for ourselves. How can we come to grips with our genetic and neurological heritage while simultaneously transcending our relational history in order to create and sustain exciting romance and nurturing love in long-term relationships? Making Love Last surveys research and theory suggesting that indeed we have the capacity and the means of achieving the lasting love we long for in our committed relationships.

Relational Interventions: Treating Borderline, Bipolar, Schizophrenic, Psychotic, and Characterological Personality Organization (2013)

Many clinicians dread working with individuals diagnosed as borderline, bipolar, schizophrenic, psychotic, and character disordered. Often labeled as "high risk" or "difficult", these relational problems and their interpersonal manifestations often require long and intense transformative therapy. In this book Dr. Hedges explains how to address the nature of personality organization in order to flow with—and eventually to enjoy—working at early developmental levels. Dr. Hedges speaks to the client's engagement/disengagement needs, using a relational process-oriented approach, so the therapist can gauge how much and what kind of therapy can be achieved at any point and time.

Facing Our Cumulative Developmental Traumas (2015)

It has now become clear that Cumulative Developmental Trauma is universal. That is, there is no way to grow up and walk the planet without being repeatedly swallowed up by emotional and relational demands from other people. When we become confused, frightened, and overwhelmed our conscious and unconscious minds seek remedies to deal with the situation. Unfortunately, many of the solutions developed in response to intrusive events turn into habitual fear reflexes that get in our way later in life, giving rise to post traumatic stress and relational inhibitions.... This book is about freeing ourselves from the cumulative effects of our life's many relational traumas and the after-effects of those traumas that continue to constrict our capacities for creative, spontaneous, and passionate living.

Relational Listening: A Handbook

Freud's singular stroke of genius can be simply stated: *When we engage with someone in an emotionally intimate relationship, the deep unconscious emotional/relational habits of both participants become interpersonally engaged and enacted thereby making them potentially available for notice, discussion, transformation, and expansion.*

This *Handbook* is the 20th book in a series edited and/or authored by Dr. Lawrence Hedges and surveys a massive clinical research project extending over 45 years and participated in by more than 400 psychotherapists in case conferences, reading groups and seminars at the Listening Perspectives Study Center and the Newport Psychoanalytic Institute in the Southern California area. The first book in the series, *Listening Perspectives in Psychotherapy* (1983), was widely praised for its comprehensive survey of 100 years of psychoanalytic studies and a 20th anniversary edition was published in 2003. But the important aspect of the book—that the studies were organized according to four different forms of relational listening according to different levels of developmental complexity—went largely unnoticed. Also generally unattended was the critical epistemological shift to perspectivalism which since that time has become better understood. The subsequent books participated in by numerous therapists expand and elaborate these *Relational Listening* perspectives for working clinicians. This *Handbook* provides not only a survey of the findings of the 45-year clinical research project but, more importantly, an overview of the seven developmental levels of relational listening that have consistently been found to provide enhanced psychotherapeutic engagement.

The Call of Darkness: A Relational Listening Approach to Suicide Intervention (2018)

The White House has declared suicide to be a national and international epidemic and has mandated suicide prevention training for educational and health workers nationwide. *The Call of Darkness* was written in response to that mandate and begins with the awareness that our ability to predict suicide is little better than chance and that at present there are no consistently reliable empirically validated treatment techniques to prevent suicide. However, in the past three decades much has been learned about the dynamics of suicide and promising treatment approaches have been advanced that are slowly yielding clinical as well as empirical results.

In this book, Dr. Hedges presents the groundbreaking work on suicidality of Freud, Jung, Menninger and Shneidman as well as the more recent work of Linehan, Kernberg, Joiner and the attachment theorists along with the features in common that these treatment approaches seem to share. He puts forth a Relational Listening approach regarding the origins of suicidality in a relational/developmental context and will consider their implications for treating, and managing suicidality. The tendencies towards blame and self-blame on the part of survivors raise issues of professional responsibility. Dr Hedges discusses accurate assessment, thorough documentation, appropriate standards of care, and liability management.

About IPI eBooks

IPI eBooks is a project of the International Psychotherapy Institute. IPI is a non-profit organization dedicated to quality training in psychodynamic psychotherapy and psychoanalysis. Through the resources of IPI, along with voluntary contributions from individuals like you, we are able to provide eBooks relevant to the field of psychotherapy at no cost to our visitors.

Our desire is to provide access to quality texts on the practice of psychotherapy in as wide a manner as possible. You are free to share our books with others as long as no alterations are made to the contents of the books. They must remain in the form in which they were downloaded.

We are always looking for authors in psychotherapy, psychoanalysis, and psychiatry that have work we would like to publish. We offer no royalties but do offer a broad distribution channel to new readers in students and practitioners of psychotherapy. If you have a potential manuscript please contact us at ebooks@theipi.org.

Other books by this publisher:

Rosemary Balsam M.D.
Sons of Passionate Mothering

By Richard D. Chessick M.D., Ph.D.
Freud Teaches Psychotherapy (Second Edition)

By Lawrence Hedges

Making Love Last: Creating and Maintaining Intimacy in Long-Term Relationships

Overcoming Our Relationship Fears

Overcoming Our Relationship Fears Workbook

Cross-Cultural Encounters: Bridging Worlds of Difference

The Relationship in Psychotherapy and Supervision

Relational Interventions

By Jerome Levin Ph.D.

Alcoholism in a Shot Glass: What You Need to Know to Understand and Treat Alcohol Abuse

The Self and Therapy

Grandmoo Goes to Rehab

Finding the Cow Within: Using Fantasy to Enrich Your Life

Childlessness: How Not Having Children Plays Out Over a Lifetime

Treating Parents of Troubled Adult Children

Living with Chronic Depression: A Rehabilitation Approach

By Fred Pine Ph.D.

Beyond Pluralism: Psychoanalysis and the Workings of Mind

By Kent Ravenscroft M.D.

Disaster Psychiatry in Haiti: Training Haitian Medical Professionals

By Joseph Reppen Ph.D. (Editor)

Beyond Freud: A Study of Modern Psychoanalytic Theorists

By David B. Sachar M.D.

Achieving Success with ADHD: Secrets from an Afflicted Professor of Medicine

By Fred Sander M.D.

Individual and Family Therapy

By Charles A. Sarnoff M.D.

Theories of Symbolism

Symbols in Psychotherapy

Symbols in Culture, Art, and Myth

By Jill Savege Scharff M.D. (Editor)

Clinical Supervision of Psychoanalytic Psychotherapy

By Jill Savege Scharff M.D. and David E. Scharff M.D.

Doctor in the House Seat: Psychoanalysis at the Theatre

By Gerald Schoenewolf Ph.D.

Psychoanalytic Centrism

By Samuel Slipp M.D.

Anti-Semitism: Its Effect on Freud and Psychoanalysis

By Imre Szecsödy M.D., Ph.D.

Supervision and the Making of the Psychoanalyst

By Vamik Volkan M.D.

Six Steps in the Treatment of Borderline Personality Organization

A Psychoanalytic Process from Beginning to its Termination

By Judith Warren Ph.D.

Reading and Therapy: Brush Up Your Shakespeare (and Proust and Hardy)

Printed in Great Britain
by Amazon

22612388R00101